Amanda Ursell's
Baby and Toddler
Food Bible

Amanda Ursell's Baby and Toddler Food Bible

YOUR ESSENTIAL GUIDE TO FEEDING YOUR CHILD FOR THEIR FIRST FOUR YEARS

Amanda Ursell

HAY HOUSE

Australia • Canada • Hong Kong • India
South Africa • United Kingdom • United States

First published and distributed in the United Kingdom by:
Hay House UK Ltd, 292B Kensal Rd, London W10 5BE. Tel.: (44) 20 8962 1230;
Fax: (44) 20 8962 1239. www.hayhouse.co.uk

Published and distributed in the United States of America by:
Hay House, Inc., PO Box 5100, Carlsbad, CA 92018-5100. Tel.: (1) 760 431 7695 or (800) 654 5126;
Fax: (1) 760 431 6948 or (800) 650 5115. www.hayhouse.com

Published and distributed in Australia by:
Hay House Australia Ltd, 18/36 Ralph St, Alexandria NSW 2015. Tel.: (61) 2 9669 4299;
Fax: (61) 2 9669 4144. www.hayhouse.com.au

Published and distributed in the Republic of South Africa by:
Hay House SA (Pty), Ltd, PO Box 990, Witkoppen 2068. Tel./Fax: (27) 11 467 8904. www.hayhouse.co.za

Published and distributed in India by:
Hay House Publishers India, Muskaan Complex, Plot No.3, B-2, Vasant Kunj, New Delhi – 110 070.
Tel.: (91) 11 4176 1620; Fax: (91) 11 4176 1630. www.hayhouse.co.in

Distributed in Canada by:
Raincoast, 9050 Shaughnessy St, Vancouver, BC V6P 6E5. Tel.: (1) 604 323 7100;
Fax: (1) 604 323 2600

© Amanda Ursell, 2011

The moral rights of the author have been asserted.

The author of this book does not dispense medical advice or prescribe the use of any technique as a form of treatment for physical or medical problems without the advice of a physician, either directly or indirectly. The intent of the author is only to offer information of a general nature to help you in your quest for emotional and spiritual wellbeing. In the event you use any of the information in this book for yourself, which is your constitutional right, the author and the publisher assume no responsibility for your actions.

A catalogue record for this book is available from the British Library.

ISBN 978-1-84850-322-9

Printed and bound in Great Britain by TJ International, Padstow, Cornwall.

MIX
Paper from
responsible sources
FSC® C013056

CONTENTS

For Coco and Freddie,
love Mummy x

ACKNOWLEDGEMENTS

My thanks to Franco for all his help with the delicious and tasty recipes that he cooks at home and that he has taught me and others to rustle up for our little ones. Thank you to Susan Brydon for her invaluable help with baby purées. I had to return to work quickly after having Freddie, and Susan introduced me to a method for making them and to a wide variety of combinations that I would never, in my sleep-deprived state, have thought of putting together. We spent many a coffee break in Italy talking over party foods and fast foods. I appreciated your input hugely, Sue-Sue. My thanks to Nina for keeping our house going. And finally a huge thank you to my dad for making mealtimes fun and my lovely mum who fed me so sensibly when I was a baby, a toddler, a child, a teenager and now when we all come over to your place. Your firm but sensible rules and down-to-earth approach to balanced meals and good nutrition and table manners stood me in good stead. Thank you, Mum.

WHY READ THIS BOOK? *

The first thing to grasp as a mother is that you know best. That is very often the reality, however at sea you may feel. Too many people try to tell you how to do things their way when you have your first baby but if you follow your own instincts (and your health visitors' guidance) you won't go far wrong. You will quickly learn to distinguish between types of cries: when for example your baby needs forty winks; when they are hungry; and when they need a cuddle for a bit of reassurance.

One of the areas where you may feel less sure of your ground is when it comes to weaning and what to feed your little ones through the toddler years. I trained as a dietitian and nutritionist and you may think that would make me 100 per cent certain of what I needed to feed my little ones. Yet, when it came to the crunch, I kept looking things up to make sure I was on the right track.

When a well-meaning relative insisted that it was fine to give my nine-month-old daughter toast with lots of butter and marmalade I knew it wasn't, but they almost convinced me I was wrong. And when another started giving her a Cornetto at ten months, telling me it was a 'bit of fun', I found it hard to wade in and say that, actually, it wasn't right at all, especially given that I was shattered from broken nights, my body was still in the grip of a hormonal rollercoaster and I was in their house, not mine. Knowing 'right' from 'wrong' about what to feed our babies and children can be fraught with these kinds of situations and knowing your facts will certainly help you through.

The list of what foods to give your baby and when to introduce them can be daunting. There seem to be so many rules: everything from food safety to allergy issues. Eggs, for instance, must be well-cooked as soft-boiled eggs carry a risk of salmonella. Certain fish need to be avoided while others should be limited to a certain number of servings per week for fear of overloading little bodies with pollutants.

With two toddlers under three, everything is fresh in my mind and I've made sure that my advice is easy to follow. The recipes are doable when you are time-short, sleep-deprived and feeling as though it is a triumph merely to get yourself and the children dressed in the morning. (You deserve a gold medal if you actually manage to put on a bit of mascara!)

I hope that you find my book useful. It is based on the experience of real mums, alongside the latest health advice. If nothing else, it will give you the ammunition you may need to explain to 'helpful' friends and relatives why you are doing things your way and not theirs. Hopefully, too, it might enable you to pass on your new ideas and recipes to other mums. It could help give them a boost if they are feeling at sea.

Chapter One

Why It Matters What and How We Feed Our Babies

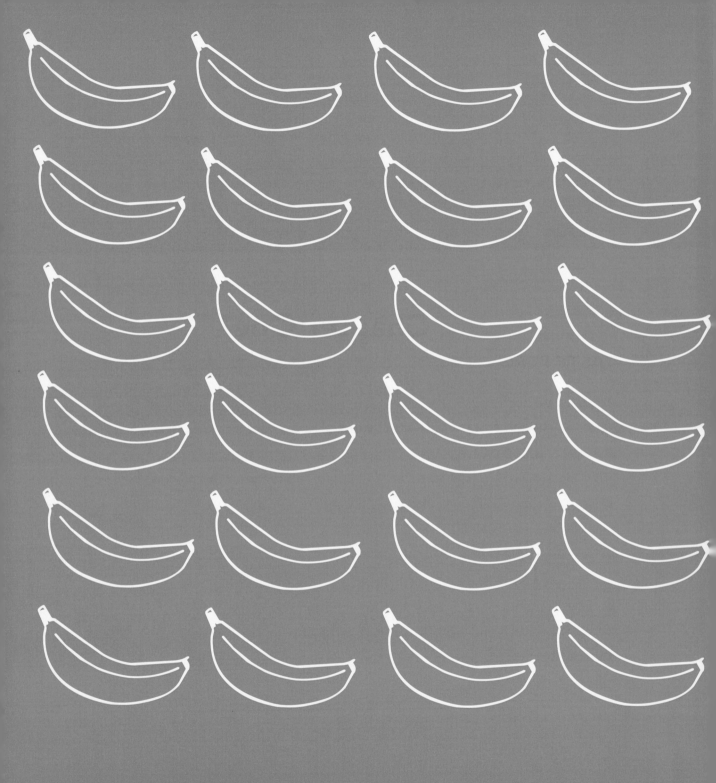

Right from the very start, what we feed our babies and how we feed them matters. You will be laying foundations for life, with habits and food preferences that will affect them developmentally, physically, emotionally and socially.

WHY 'REAL' FOOD COUNTS *

TASTE PERCEPTION

All babies are born with an innate preference for sweet foods. This is just as well because breast milk is sweet-tasting and is the safe, nutritionally complete food for their initial needs. I remember seeing photos at a lecture of a brand spanking-new baby who was given the tiniest amount of a naturally sweet-tasting solution on her tongue. The expression on her face was captured in a photograph: undoubtedly pleasure. Then she was given a bitter-tasting substance (I can only assume that this little baby had research scientists for parents who knew what they were doing!). This time, the baby's face crumpled with displeasure. When given a sour taste, the baby puckered her lips as if she were sucking lemons. Interestingly, had she been given a salty taste she would not have reacted because babies can't discern saltiness until they are a few months old. (It is good to know that you are not born with this preference.)

While we are born with a liking of sweet foods and a dislike of bitter-tasting foods, tastes develop and mature so that the latter can be successfully introduced gradually to meals. We can incorporate sweet foods in a moderate way too. It is here where parents play a large role in shaping their children's future palates, their food and drink choices and, in turn, their nutritional intake. Their future health is to a great extent in your hands.

From the earliest stages of weaning, if we feed our growing children fresh, healthy and tasty food in a safe and happy environment we are encouraging a lifetime of healthy eating. A meal (even a purée) eaten when calm and happy can help to determine whether it is enjoyed and therefore wanted again. A stressful, unhappy environment can equally put a child off food or drink.

It is hard to know where the taste preferences we are born with end and the learning and conditioning to enjoy others begin. We do know that the best we can do is offer healthy food in a positive situation at mealtimes. That way, it gets the best possible chance of being eaten and enjoyed. Sorry to bang the message home but it is an important one. If you serve real food from the word go then your babies are more likely to grow into children who expect to eat real, tasty food. If all they know is the taste of processed food from jars and packets, doled out in an unsympathetic environment, it shouldn't be a surprise that all they want is processed food in the future. We are creatures of habit, after all. Eating these foods in this kind of environment can also lay down the foundations for fussy eating (see page 32). However, the chances are that you won't need this information if you appreciate how vital it is to establish positive habits from the start.

If children grow up eating ready-meals and junk food they are likely to be heading down a track that leads to being overweight or obese in later life with a higher risk of Type 2 diabetes, heart disease and stroke. It is hard to imagine that this is the path any parent wants their child to follow. Taking care how you feed them in early life can help to prevent this path being trodden. None of us wants our children to die before us from diseases that are food-related and preventable.

THINGS TO THINK ABOUT WHEN PREPARING BABIES', TODDLERS' AND CHILDREN'S MEALS *

MAKING FOOD TASTE GOOD

Generally, the way to make food taste good is to prepare and cook as much of your own as possible. You do not need fantastic cooking skills. You just need to know some basics and the rest you can pick up as you go along.

Buying seasonal and locally produced food can sometimes help to get the best-tasting food but this is not always the case. Sometimes, supermarkets with a fast turnover of, say, fruits and vegetables can compete very well on this front. You need to test out your local area and see which is best in your view.

Avoiding overcooking also helps on the taste front (overcooked broccoli, sprouts and cabbage, for example, taste much more bitter than those cooked for a minimal time), as does being prepared to put in a bit of time and effort. Most of the recipes in this book are designed to be quick and easy. However, some do need a bit of commitment in the first place such as making up a batch of tasty stock or home-made tomato sauce. The benefit is that these basics can be made in batches and frozen, then used in a plethora of dishes, ultimately cutting down on work in the kitchen.

Being prepared to give toddlers the kind of food that you are serving for yourselves and the rest of the family (with less salt and sugar) is, in my view, a key step in ensuring that your children grow up on tasty food. Otherwise, it's all too easy to fall into the ready-meal and fussy-eaters trap.

WHAT IT FEELS LIKE

Food comes in many shapes and textures. When you first begin to wean your baby, the conventional wisdom (baby-led weaning aside) is to offer food in a puréed form and to alter the consistency gradually, becoming thicker as you progress. Next, lumps and finger foods are introduced, followed by mashed, then chopped food, until finally meals of normal consistency are eaten.

It is important that, as children move through these stages, they are introduced to as many age-appropriate textures as possible so that they avoid becoming hooked on one particular consistency. This can lead to fussy eating, with a child getting 'stuck' on soft food, for instance. This does mean you will need to plan meals so that if, for example, you are serving pasta, which is soft, then it is a good idea to have something crunchy elsewhere in the meal. This could be achieved with baby sweetcorn on the side or some crunchy apple afterwards.

WHAT IT LOOKS LIKE

It is often said that we eat with our eyes. Try to introduce lots of colours when planning meals. Children love bright colours so you may as well make the most of this with colourful vegetables and fruits. It is not simply a case of encouraging little ones to 'eat their greens'. Oranges (in carrots and mangoes), reds (in tomatoes and strawberries), yellows (in sweetcorn and bananas) and purples (in aubergines and blueberries) are just as important and will give a vibrant and appealing edge to meals. Think about it from your own perspective: nothing could be more boring and uninspiring to look at than a plate with white fish, mashed potato and leeks in white sauce. Baked cod with orange-coloured mashed sweet potato and carrots, some peas and ratatouille is another thing altogether.

HOW IT SMELLS

When shaping likes and dislikes it is worth remembering just how important it is that food smells nice. Odours are not only breathed in through the nose, when sniffing a ripe strawberry for example, but move via the mouth to smelling centres in our brains as well. Our perception of flavour is a combination of how food smells from these two sources and how it tastes (whether it is salty, sweet, bitter or sour) when we chew it.

Smell is a powerful sense but we are not born with preferences for how things smell. We gradually learn about smells we do not like. Most of us know how cabbage smells when it is overcooked: it is pretty offputting. Cutting the cooking time changes the smell completely to a softer and more pleasant aroma. And we all know how lovely and warming is the smell of scones and bread baking in the oven. If you can help a child grow up used to the smell of healthy dishes cooking in your kitchen it may well reinforce a desire for them. Opening jars of baby food or ready-meals day in day out simply does not have the same effect.

I once had a lecturer who said that if you allow your children to eat badly it is tantamount to child abuse. I thought he was exaggerating wildly but when I came to think of it he had a point: bad diets lead to bad health and, potentially, an early death. I often think about this when I'm feeling worn out by cooking yet another meal. It spurs me on to get out the chopping board and think about how I can offer nice-tasting, lovely nice-looking meals that my children will want to tuck into.

The first summer of my daughter Coco's life I spent in Italy with her Daddy, Franco, and his mum and dad (or Nono and Nonina to Coco). The first day when I opened a pot of baby food I'd brought with us to feed her while we were travelling, Nonina stopped me in my tracks.

'Why do you give her that?' (said with a strong Italian accent and a disdainful downward glance at the pot, which Coco was clearly not enjoying that much).

'She should be having this!' (holding up a bowl of pastina, the tiny star-shaped pasta made with real chicken stock, delicious pieces of chicken, carrot and onion).

'Well, it's, er, I thought it was safer ...'

Nonina looked even more put out. 'My mother gave me this as a child. I gave my Franc' this as a child. Are you saying the food I gave my Franc' is not good? And the food my Mother gave me is not good?'

'Eh, no ... it's just ...'

And with that, the dish under Coco's nose was whisked away and in its place a bowl of pastina was lovingly put down. And, of course, Coco ate the lot. With relish. From this point on I decided that, whenever possible, I would serve my children honest, home-cooked food. I don't always manage it but I do my best.

Chapter Two

So What Do My Baby and Toddler Need Nutritionally?

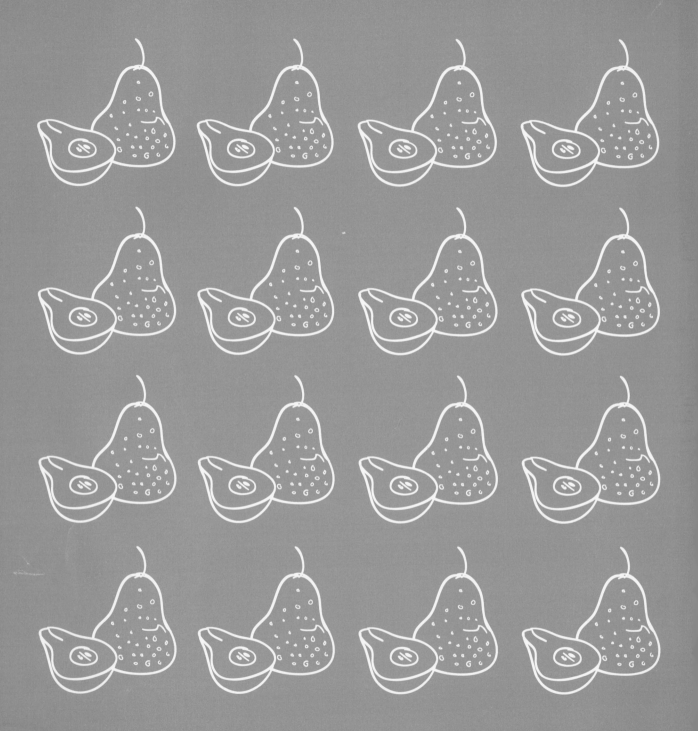

The current advice is that you should try to breastfeed your baby for at least the first six months. If you are not breastfeeding, but bottle feeding instead, the same length of time applies. It is thought that persevering until this age is good: the risk of tummy upsets, food intolerances*and allergies is lessened due to your baby's digestive and immune systems being stronger and more able to cope with new foods. From a practical point of view, a six-month-old baby is likely to be sitting up so that they can be fed in a highchair. And, by then, most babies will want to start chewing.

The process of weaning takes you from around six months of age into the first year of your child's life. This is a time when every part of their body, including the brain and other organs, skin, tissues, muscles and bones, grow quickly in weight and size. Not surprisingly, a child of this age has high nutritional needs.

NUTRITIONAL REASONS TO START WEANING *

At six months of age a baby is not able to get all the nutrients it needs from milk so needs to start building up a repertoire of foods to help plug the gaps. Milk remains a major source of nourishment until about one year of age (breast milk being offered regularly throughout the weaning process or 500–600ml formula daily). You are starting the process of, quite literally, 'weaning' them off their total nutritional dependence on milk but you need to do it gradually.

REASONS A BABY BEGINS TO NEED FOOD OTHER THAN MILK

Energy: growing babies and toddlers (toddlers are defined as being 1–3 years old) need semi-solid and solid foods to meet their energy needs. Getting insufficient energy will stunt physical and mental development at all stages of childhood.

Iron: breast milk is low in this mineral but, in the first six months, babies get by on the stores they build up in their bodies during their mother's pregnancy. After that, these stores are running low and they need additional supplies of iron via food. Traditionally, meat and fish have been suggested as later-stage weaning foods. However, the American Dietetic Association says it is fine to introduce these foods from early months of weaning as part of purées to help a baby get enough of this vital nutrient. As well as meat and fish, other foods that provide iron include pulses, such as peas and lentils, dried apricots, plus a little in dark-green vegetables. Baby milk formulas have added iron, as do toddler milks designed for 1–3 year olds. Over 80 per cent of toddlers have been found in surveys to have a low intake of iron and one in eight is actually anaemic due to poor iron intake.

Insufficient amounts of iron can affect learning and development at all stages of childhood.

Vitamin D: breast milk is low in vitamin D and stores will be running out by six months. It is found in few foods so, unless you are giving your baby 500ml of formula that contains vitamin D, a specific infant vitamin drop formulation containing this nutrient is advised. Although a few foods do contain this vitamin, such as fortified breakfast cereals and oily fish (such as sardines, salmon, pilchards and trout), the cereals aren't suitable for babies in the first six months of weaning and the fish is usually too strong-tasting to appeal. After one year of age, if you have moved to cow's milk (and are not giving 500–600ml toddler formula) a child usually still needs vitamin drops. Ask your health visitor for advice regarding supplementation.

A lack of vitamin D can lead to rickets and general poor bone formation throughout childhood.

Vitamin A: similarly, vitamin A is needed too. Surveys have shown that 50 per cent of toddlers have low intakes of vitamin A. As with vitamin D, unless having a formula which is fortified with vitamin A, vitamin drops are advised. In fact, as mentioned, these are advised for many children until the age of five. Seek advice from your health visitor. Some vitamin A can be made in our bodies from beta carotene, the lovely vibrant orange colour found in carrots, mangoes and apricots, as well as some dark-green vegetables such as spinach and darker-coloured cabbage (the green pigments disguise it).

A lack of vitamin A affects eye health and mental development.

Vitamin C: another vitamin not found in breast milk, this nutrient can also be obtained from children's vitamin drops. Vitamin C is needed in the diet after the age of six months when stores accumulated from pregnancy will be running low. Some first weaning foods that provide it include sweet potatoes and papaya. Later foods include citrus fruits and dark-green vegetables such as spinach and peppers.

A really bad lack of vitamin C can lead to scurvy. This is rare in developed countries but meeting daily needs will help to ensure that your baby grows and develops well, especially with respect to their immune system and skin.

Super-nutrients: so-called super-nutrients, such as lutein (the yellow pigment in spinach, red peppers, broccoli and watercress) and beta carotene (the orange colour in carrots and mangoes), do not actually have specific deficiency diseases associated with them. We do know, however, that lutein, for example, appears to helps protect us from sun damage.

The eyes of infants and young children are especially prone to ultraviolet damage. Thus, building up stores of lutein is potentially important for eye health.

Omega 3 essential fats: you do get some in breast milk, depending on the mother's diet, and there are some infant formulas that contain them. Omega 3 essential fats are just that: essential. You need to try to make sure that your baby is getting some in their weaning foods and throughout childhood as they are crucial for development of sight and hearing. You can find these essential fats in foods like oily fish and eggs laid by chickens that have had omega 3 (EPA and DHA) added to their diet. Omega 3s from all plant oils, such as flax-seed oil, have to be converted in the body into a usable form. This process is not very effective in humans so it is important that the right kind of omega 3s are provided.

A lack of omega 3s may lead to less than optimal development of both sight and hearing and may affect learning abilities throughout childhood.

Fibre: as milk has no fibre, of course, the introduction of solids is important from this point of view as well. The digestive system needs fibre to 'get it going' and this applies to babies over six months as well as toddlers and adults. Weaning babies will get plenty of fibre from the small amounts of vegetables and fruits gradually introduced and then from cereal foods. There is absolutely no need to feed them 'high fibre' things like wheatbran!

A lack of fibre, once your baby moves into the toddler stage, may lead to constipation so it is important to get the balance right.

> **As weaning progresses your little one will move from being a baby to growing into a toddler. It is important to remember that, until they are older, children usually cannot manage to eat large amounts of food at one go. This means that they need meals and snacks that are full of nutrients: full-fat dairy foods, meat, eggs and pulses with some starchy foods, fruits and vegetables to go with them.**

WHAT INFANTS AND TODDLERS DO NOT NEED NUTRITIONALLY

Added salt and processed foods: children under seven months should be having less than 1g of salt per day. This means no added salt and no foods that give us salt. From seven months to a year, they should be having a maximum of 1g of salt per day. From one to three years, they should have no more than 2g daily and from four to six, no more than 3g per day. To give this a sense of perspective, most adults eat around 9g per day (although they should only have a maximum of 6g). This means that no salt should be added to any weaning foods and care should be taken to avoid processed foods as much as possible.

> Whatever age your child might be, it is worth being aware that bread and breakfast cereals are big contributors of salt so don't over-rely on these foods.
>
> 1 slice of medium slice bread = 0.4g salt
> 45g bowl of Shreddies with milk = 0.5g salt
> 1 mini pitta bread = 0.3g salt
> 30g bowl of Rice Krispies with milk = 0.6g salt
> 1 x 30g matchbox serving of cheddar = 0.6g salt

Foods like porridge oats, oatmeal, rice, pasta and potatoes naturally contain virtually no salt and are good to include in babies' and toddlers' diets. With the exception of pasta, they are not wheat-based foods either. I always try to mix and match the carbohydrates I give my little ones so that they have just one meal a day containing wheat. There is a view that wheat intolerance may develop when wheat is over-used. Keeping it to once a day seems like a sensible approach and also, of course, means that you have lots of variety at mealtimes.

While no salt should be added to any food for a child under the age of one, if you make sure that your children are not overdoing the kinds of foods in the list above, there is a little scope to use a very small and controlled amount in seasoning. Check the Main Meals section (page 177) to learn more about this.

Sugar: should not be added to weaning foods because it provides energy (calories) but no nutrients. You need to pack as many nutrients as you can into the calories that are eaten, rather than filling up on empty calories. Once your child has been weaned, it is still sensible to keep sugar to a minimum because toddlers and young children are growing rapidly and still need plenty of nutrient-rich foods rather than filling up on low-nutrient, sugar-packed offerings. And, of course, you do not want to ruin their teeth.

It is hard to ban all sweet foods from children's diets because it is the one taste they usually absolutely love, not least because breast and formula feeds taste quite sweet. From an evolutionary point of view, sweet-tasting foods were the ones that were generally 'safe' to eat, while bitter ones tended to be those that were more likely to be poisonous or in some way harmful. Expecting children not to like sweet-tasting foods is going against nature.

What we need to do as parents is to provide sweetness in ways that also add some goodness rather than allowing children to satisfy their tendencies with boiled sweets and sugar-laden puddings, which add nothing to their diets nutritionally. The puddings in my book have been chosen because they are a happy medium. They provide some sweetness and lots of goodness. And because they are eaten at mealtimes they are less likely to cause tooth decay than sugary foods eaten between meals. One good way of introducing sweet-tasting but healthy snacks is to offer fruits like ripe mangoes, banana, pineapple or apricots between meals, although it's always worth brushing teeth if you can after dried fruit snacks. Check out the chapter on snacking (p.158).

Too much fibre: the term 'muesli-belt malnutrition' was coined by scientists concerned about overly zealous mums who they feared were feeding their children too many wholegrain foods to the point that they were so full from their fibre-rich diet that they had no room for those nutrient-dense foods needed for their general growth and wellbeing.

It is important to strike a balance. While it is a good idea to gradually introduce wholemeal bread and wholegrain cereals, there is no need to go over the top with dense mueslis and added bran. 'Be sensible' is the key message here.

Low-fat milk: children over two are recommended to have semi-skimmed milk and only to switch to skimmed once they are five (and if they are otherwise well nourished). From two until five they are thought to need the extra calories provided by the semi-skimmed.

Note:

- Infants under one should not be given honey. It can contain spores of botulinum, which may lead to serious and even fatal food poisoning if eaten by babies whose systems are not able to deal with this toxin.

- If you wean before six months of age, no soft or unpasteurised cheese should be given, no nuts or seeds, no cows' milk, eggs, wheat or gluten-containing foods (bread, cereals or pasta, for example) and no fish or shellfish.

- Babies of six months to a year should not be given undercooked or raw eggs (this is true for toddlers and young children too, see below). The yolks should be solid.

- Some fish are high in methyl mercury, which may affect a child's mental development adversely. For this reason, young children (as well as women of child-bearing age and those who are pregnant) should not eat swordfish, marlin, shark or the white-fleshed albacore tuna. I would also be wary of most shellfish because it is prone to carrying food-poisoning bugs.

Vegetarian babies

The diets of vegetarian babies need special care and attention. It is likely that vegetarian mums take a lot of care with their own diets and probably know quite a bit about nutrition. But because babies have different nutritional needs to adults it is worth brushing up on their requirements as well as your own, and those of older infants too. This is important because, while adult vegetarian diets are often healthier, being less energy-dense and higher in fibre, this is not a good combination for babies.

Ideally, a vegetarian baby needs two good sources of protein a day from well-cooked eggs, soya-based foods or pulses like chick peas, lentils, haricot and butter beans. Vitamin C-rich foods like peppers, berries and citrus fruits need to be given within the same meal to help the iron in these protein foods be absorbed. (Peppers can be cooked and puréed and the juice of citrus fruits added to purées.)

It is especially important to give vitamin drops to babies who are on a vegetarian diet, so do talk to your health visitor about this.

Vegan babies

Please, please, if you want to bring your baby up as a vegan, see your health visitor and a Registered Dietitian to get some sound advice. It is not recommended that babies are brought up as vegans but, if you absolutely insist on doing so, please get the best advice possible to ensure that your child grows and thrives.

WHAT TODDLERS NEED

At this age, children are still growing very quickly and are usually very active. They need plenty of calories and nutrients from healthy foods (not biscuits, sweets, crisps and sweetened drinks) as well as drinking water regularly to remain well hydrated. A healthy and varied diet should provide most nutrients your toddler needs although most do still need vitamin drops. Check this out with your health visitor.

Remember to include these sorts of foods every day:

- Milk and dairy foods – these provide protein, vitamins and minerals (especially calcium) and are a good source of calories for growing children. Have several servings a day. This could be a glass of milk, milk on breakfast cereals, a portion of yoghurt or a serving of cheese.

  One toddler-size portion is 100–120ml cows' or toddler milk, a 125ml pot of yoghurt, 2–4 tablespoons grated cheese in a sandwich or on a pizza, or 3–6 tablespoons of custard or milk pudding.

- Meat, fish, eggs, beans, peas and lentils – these are good for protein, and also some vitamins and minerals. You can give boys up to four portions of oily fish a week (such as mackerel, salmon and sardines) but it is best to give girls no more than two portions a week. (This is because oily fish contain pollutants, such as dioxins, which get stored in the body and may affect their future development. Personally, I don't give my little boy more than two servings either.) Give your toddlers protein-rich foods in at least two of their main meals.

  One toddler-size portion is 2–4 tablespoons of ground, chopped or cubed lean meat, fish or poultry; ½–1 whole egg, 2–4 whole or mashed pulses like peas, beans, lentils, hummus or dahl; ½–1 tablespoon peanut butter or 1–2 tablespoons of ground or chopped nuts.

- Bread and other cereals – these and other starchy foods (such as rice, pasta, breakfast cereals, potatoes, yams and sweet potatoes) provide calories, vitamins, minerals and fibre. Give your toddler cereal-based foods at every meal but try to choose those without added salt as much as possible. I also vary the types given so that they are not having wheat-based starchy foods at every meal. For example: toast at breakfast; a rice-based dish at lunch; and a potato-based meal for dinner.

  One toddler-size portion is ½–1 wholegrain or white breads, muffin, roll or pancake; 3–6 heaped tablespoons wholegrain or fortified breakfast cereals without a sugar coating; 5–8 tablespoons of hot cereals like porridge, made with milk; 2–5 cooked tablespoons rice or 1–3 tablespoons cooked pasta; ½–2 crispbreads or 1–3 crackers.

- Fruit and vegetables – these contain vitamin C and other protective vitamins and minerals as well as fibre and a plethora of super-nutrients. Give your toddlers fruit or vegetables at every meal, aiming for five a day in total. Remember, however, that a portion is only the amount they could hold in the palm of their hand – it is not five adult-sized portions!

  One toddler-size portion is for example ¼–½ apple, orange, pear or banana; 3–10 small berries or grapes; 2–4 tablespoons freshly cooked, stewed or mashed fruit; 1–3 tablespoons raw or cooked vegetables, especially dark green, orange and yellow ones.

Note on portion sizes: there are no set portion sizes for toddlers but those above are given as a guide. Toddlers have a wide variation in the quantities eaten at meals and snacks, depending on which stage they are in their toddlerhood. Again as a guide, smaller, younger toddlers will probably eat about the amounts given at the lower end of these ranges while older toddlers will edge towards the upper ranges.

Snacks

In addition to three nutritious and balanced main meals, your toddler will benefit from two (and in some cases three) small snacks between meals as well. This may sound like a lot but your little ones' tummies are still quite small and they can't 'stock up' with big portions, in the way adults can, at main meals. Having regular, nutritious snacks helps them get from one meal to the next without getting grumpy and tired but snacks also provide a really good opportunity to top up with vital nutrients. Check out my nutritious snacks section (p.160).

Nutritious and regular snacks are also invaluable to help you through fussy-eating stages. See my chapter on fussy-eaters (p.29).

What toddlers should not be eating

I have already warned against undercooked or raw eggs, fish high in methyl mercury and most shellfish (see p.21).

Other foods to avoid include whole grapes, whole nuts and popcorn as they can cause choking. Cut up grapes and other small fruits; with nuts, try crushing and including in foods like yoghurt to reduce the risk of them catching in the throats of little ones. (Obviously nuts are not suitable for children with nut allergies.)

You can give semi-skimmed milk to children between two to five years of age if they are eating and growing well (see p.20). If you have any doubts, check with your health visitor.

While very small amounts of salt may help a dish to taste more appealing and very small amounts may be added to certain dishes (as long as they don't also contain ingredients such as cheese and bacon, which add more salt), it should, on the whole, be avoided wherever possible (see p.18). It is also really important to avoid as much processed food as possible because 75 per cent of the salt in our diets comes from that source. As I said before, I would be careful not to give too much bread, pitta or breakfast cereals as the salt in these foods can add up. Porridge, rice, potatoes, couscous or plain noodles are all good alternatives and are naturally virtually salt free. If you want to use ready-to-eat breakfast cereals, opt for low-salt versions like Oatibix and Weetabix.

The same goes for sugar. Let them have a bit of sugar in their puddings but avoid sweets, sugary drinks and sweet snacks between meals. If children don't have them they tend not to expect them. My advice is not to have them in the house, then you won't get pestered. If we do have treats we have them when we are out. That way, Coco knows that they don't come back to the house with us so I am not nagged constantly to get things from the cupboard.

Peanuts: check out my chapter on allergies to find out what to do about peanuts (p.47).

Vegetarian toddlers

The same advice applies to toddlers and young children as weaning babies. You must take really good care to provide well-balanced meals and not to go overboard with fibre.

LITTLE CHILDREN (3 YEARS AND OLDER)

Again, the same advice applies with small children as for toddlers. They are able to eat a bit more at mealtimes but, essentially, they are still little and can benefit from three balanced meals and two healthy snacks.

All children thrive on routine and the one really good thing about it is that it does help prevent and deal with fussy eating.

An organisation called the Infant and Toddler Forum has issued a ten-step guide for healthy toddlers to help establish good habits for health, growth and development.

This can be found by logging on to www.littlepeoplesplates.co.uk

In summary, the points it makes are:

- **Eat together as a family and make mealtimes relaxed and happy occasions with all the family eating the foods you would like your toddler to eat (taking into account appropriate salt and sugar levels and serving sizes).**

- You decide on the nutritious foods to offer your toddler but let your toddler decide how much they eat, never insisting that they finish everything on their plate.

- Offer foods from the important food groups mentioned above every day to help provide them with the right mix of nutrients.

- Have a routine of three meals and two to three snacks a day and don't allow all-day grazing on food.

- Offer 6–8 drinks a day, giving them in a cup or beaker and sticking mostly to water in around 100–120ml servings. Don't give tea, coffee, constant milk drinks, sugary drinks or undiluted fruit juices.

- Give vitamins A and D each day, choosing a supplement suitable for toddlers because most do not get sufficient of these vitamins in their diets for strong immunity and growth.

- Respect your toddler's tastes and preferences and don't force them to eat foods they loathe.

- Reward your toddler with your attention but never give food or drink as a reward or treat or for comfort.

- Limit fried foods, crisps, biscuits, cakes and sweet foods.

- Encourage at least an hour of active play each day and about 12 hours' sleep.

Chapter Three

Fussy Eaters

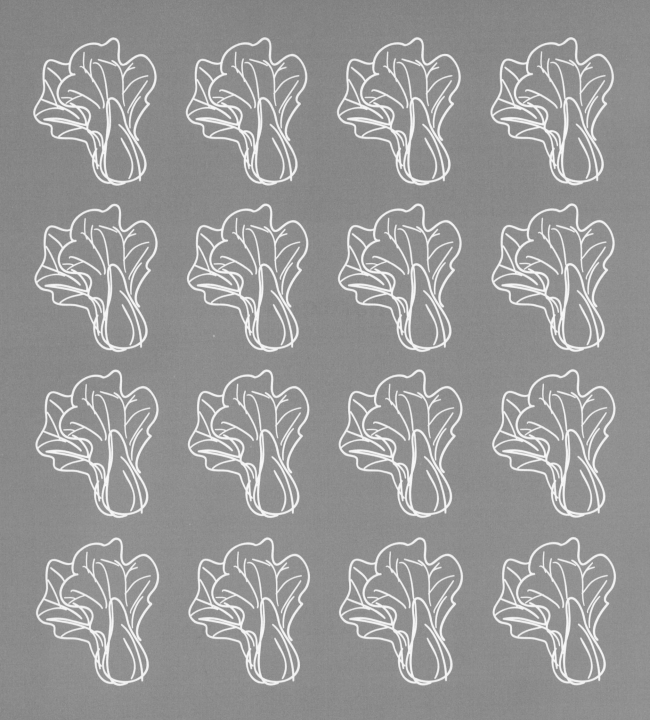

If you are reading this book as a new mum or a new mum-to-be, then fussy eaters are something you may have come across in newspaper articles, on nanny programmes on the television or perhaps through friends or relatives who are dealing with the problem. You won't have lived through the experience yourself. The hope is, you will not have to. I have no research to prove this, but I would take a bet that the number of fussy eaters growing up in countries where food is scarce is almost non-existent. If you do not have enough food you do not have the luxury to be picky. You eat what is available.

I sometimes wonder if, perhaps, fussy eaters are something we have somehow taught our children to become. Before you fire off an angry email to me, please do read this chapter! You may end up agreeing, if only a little bit, with this point of view.

THE 'OLD' DAYS

When I was growing up there were no such things as child-led meal preferences and there were no alternatives on offer if my brother or I did not fancy the meal my Mum had made. We simply ate what we were given. Obviously there were times when we went off our food for a bit: when we were teething, tired, feeling poorly, worried about something and so on, but there was no room for tantrums and games. As a result, we tended not to try and wrap my mum around our little fingers and insist on only eating foods of a certain colour or texture. We certainly didn't demand an alternative to the meal she had prepared.

My mum says that she didn't serve foods that she knew we loathed. For instance, my brother simply didn't like peas and, because there were other vegetables he did enjoy, Mum saw no point in forcing him to have them. (Now, oddly enough, he eats them happily.) On the whole, though, my mum says that we were not pandered to. It was also very much true of most of our young friends who we had meals with after school or visited at the weekend.

I think fussy eating is, in part, a modern-day phenomenon; one which may have come about due to the way we bring our children up. Many of us are prepared to run a canteen-style service in our kitchens where we ask little people what they want, making one meal for them, then are happy to run around making another if they don't eat it. We can't really blame our children for thinking this is normal, so they gradually take things a step further each time and begin to use meals as a way of exerting control in the household.

EXCEPTION TO THE RULE

There is one exception you should be aware of so that you know how to handle it if the phase does occur. We lived through it with Coco and probably will again with Freddie. It is called 'neophagia', which means 'fear of the new'. It often occurs soon after toddlers have begun walking and can roam around, checking out their environment. Judy More, a dietitian who is an expert in childhood eating patterns, says it is probably a survival mechanism to help curb a young toddler's natural interest in picking up anything they can find and trying to eat it. After all, interesting-looking berries on a bush could actually be poisonous so neophagia may well be a mechanism that evolved to help us survive.

If a child does go through this stage, they are likely to clamp their mouth shut, as Coco did, and shake their head, refusing to try a food they do not recognise. My daughter started walking at nine months and neophagia duly kicked in at 14 months, manifesting itself as a point-blank refusal to eat anything other than plain pasta and yoghurt. It can be alarming when you hit a fussy-eating phase like this but I found that having this information about neophagia up my sleeve helped hugely. I did get stressed but tried not to let my daughter see it. I simply kept on reintroducing foods to her plate as part of family mealtimes. I always made sure that she could see me eating these foods to give her the sense that they were safe to try. Perhaps because of this, and the fact that she had been used to eating normal family food before it occurred, she got through the phase pretty quickly.

The key is not to worry too much. My daughter kept growing normally so she was obviously eating enough pasta and yoghurt, although we thought it unbelievably dull and not exactly a great mix of nutrients. Now she is happy to try most things she is offered. Of course, she doesn't like everything, but the general rule in our house is that you have a try before deciding.

REDUCING THE CHANCES OF A TODDLER BECOMING A FUSSY EATER

Most experts who work in the area of fussy eating will tell you the same thing. Children are less likely to turn into fussy eaters if they are weaned on real, home-cooked food (rather than exclusively on jars of baby food) and if they eat the same food at the same time as the other people around them, whether it is with you, the family, or their carer.

Making your own purées or eating meals together may sound like it won't fit in with your lifestyle, and maybe it won't, but it is worth investing time and effort to establish this pattern and altering your routines in order to do so. Doing it early on can save hours of heartache and tantrums later and actually help your little one grow up to eat well-balanced, regular meals and enjoy a wide variety of foods.

FOOD FADS VERSUS LIKES AND DISLIKES

Although it can take up to ten times of introducing a new food to a little one before they will accept it, I think it is worth being aware that children, like grown-ups, do have some genuine likes and dislikes. There are some foods that they will simply never want to eat.

Some children do perceive bitter flavours more acutely than others (a genetic trait that follows into adulthood). These children will not be able to tolerate bitter-tasting foods such as Brussels sprouts, watercress and broccoli. If your child looks pained when tasting such foods they may be 'super-tasters' for whom such foods are simply too overpowering. If this is the case, try cooking these vegetables for a minimum time adding milk (for example, by using broccoli and milk to make a soup). However, it could be that you are going to have to let the broccoli thing go and make sure that they have a good variety of other vegetables instead. The best-known broccoli hater is probably the first George Bush. When President, he told chefs to take the vegetable off the menus at The White House and on his jet, Air Force One, he even interrupted a press conference on an important defence issue to answer a journalist's question on the subject. He said that he'd implemented the ban because he didn't like broccoli as a child when his mom made him eat it, and he still didn't like it so, now that he was President, he was banning it!

Other children have quirky little traits around some foods, which seem to come from nowhere and are probably best accommodated in the knowledge that they will probably grow out of them. You don't want mealtimes to become a battle-ground. My daughter, for instance, does not like her food to be coated in sauces. My son, on the other hand, doesn't seem to mind. Given that it matters to Coco and not to Freddie, I tend to avoid dishes like cauliflower or macaroni cheese. Happily, though, it does seem, now that she's nearly three, that she is starting to grow out of this particular preference.

My daughter also went through a short phase of having a 'thing' about only having a certain brand of Greek yoghurt. When a different one appeared on the table she just didn't want it. With a bit of subterfuge we got around that one and now she's fine with whichever brand appears. This could have been another manifestation of neophagia I guess.

My friend's little boy had a similar phase when he stopped wanting pineapple smoothies, which he had previously loved. As my friend eventually discovered, this sudden aversion came about because the drink reminded him of his baby brother being sick. It is worth being aware that this kind of negative association can happen with all manner of foods and drinks and is also quite a common phase, tending to occur around three years of age. It is worth exploring with your toddler why they may have gone off a previously well-loved food and to try to work through these things without piling on any pressure.

It is also important to bear in mind that if your child is filling up on drinks and snacks between meals they are unlikely to feel hungry at mealtimes. As a result, they may reject food not because they are being fussy but simply because they are still full. Strangely, it is also true that if they go too long without sustenance they may not fancy eating when they do get to their mealtime. Be aware of this and start to monitor just how much your child is snacking and drinking between meals, when they last ate and so on, and adjust things accordingly.

Also consider what is going on around them. If my children can hear the noise of a television in another room they find it distracting and difficult to concentrate on their meal. This is not due to fussiness; it is because they simply cannot focus on the task in hand. Other mums agree that you need to switch off the television, turn off the computer and try to calm the area where children are eating to help avoid them rejecting food.

There are other things that can affect a child's appetite at mealtimes. The first is if they are constipated. In the case of one of my daughter's friends, it took a trip to the GP as well as a cranial osteopath to sort things out. While she was having the problem she often rejected meals as it was uncomfortable to eat and her appetite had been suppressed. The second reason for loss of appetite can be if a child has too little iron in their diet and has become sub-clinically or fully anaemic. If your toddler or small child seems abnormally lethargic, it is worth talking with your GP and voicing your concerns. I give both of my children two drinks of toddler milk a day because, as hard as I try with their diets, I am not convinced that they get enough iron from their foods on a daily basis. It is just an extra insurance policy and, happily, lack of energy is not a problem with which we have had to cope.

Try to keep mealtimes to a manageable timescale. Expecting a little one to sit for ages is not reasonable and they may reject pudding simply because it has taken so long to arrive. You don't want to find yourselves racing through mealtimes but it is hard for a small child to sit in a chair, without getting restless, for more than about 15 minutes when really little and 20 minutes when a bit older. The fact is that small children's mealtimes need effective time management. If buying a house is all about location, location, location, getting children's mealtimes right is all about planning, planning, planning. If you do, the chances are you will save yourselves a lot of heart-aches, tantrums and future problems with food fads.

THE BOTTOM LINE

The bottom line with these little blips is that most toddlers grow out of them and, if they are growing normally, it is best to try to remain as calm as possible and to stick with business as usual: home-cooked meals, a clear and regular routine, and sitting down to eat together. Children learn by emulating you, their brothers and sisters and other people with whom they regularly eat. They usually get back on track with patience and time. But remember, if they see you being picky and weird around food and mealtimes, you can hardly blame them if they become so too. If you know you have some odd habits, then there can be no greater motivation for sorting them out than avoiding passing them on to the next generation.

Finally, I suggest that if your child does point-blank refuse to eat (and it is clear that there is no good reason for it other than trying it on with manipulation and control tactics), do try taking them down from the table without offering an alternative. If they have a regular routine of meal/snack/meal/snack they will be fine if you do. Yes, they will be missing a meal but, if they are growing normally and you know that they will have a nutritious snack offered within a couple of hours, it is not going to do them any harm. The chances are, if you do this a few times, they will stop pretty quickly once they have worked out the consequences and see that you are not giving in to their demands.

As a parent, armed with a little knowledge, you should quite quickly be able to tell the difference between genuine reasons for food refusal – those issues that really do concern and upset them – and when they are playing up.

IF THINGS PERSIST

On talking with experts, I learned one slightly concerning yet highly motivating point. If you don't get serious fussy eating and peculiar demands ironed out by the time a child is four, it is pretty difficult to change things thereafter. Put in the effort now and you should be making your own and your children's lives a lot easier, not to say healthier, in the years to come.

If you do have young or older children who are stuck in the rut of fussy eating, ask your GP to refer you to a Registered Dietitian to get some individual advice.

Chapter Four

Allergies and Intolerances

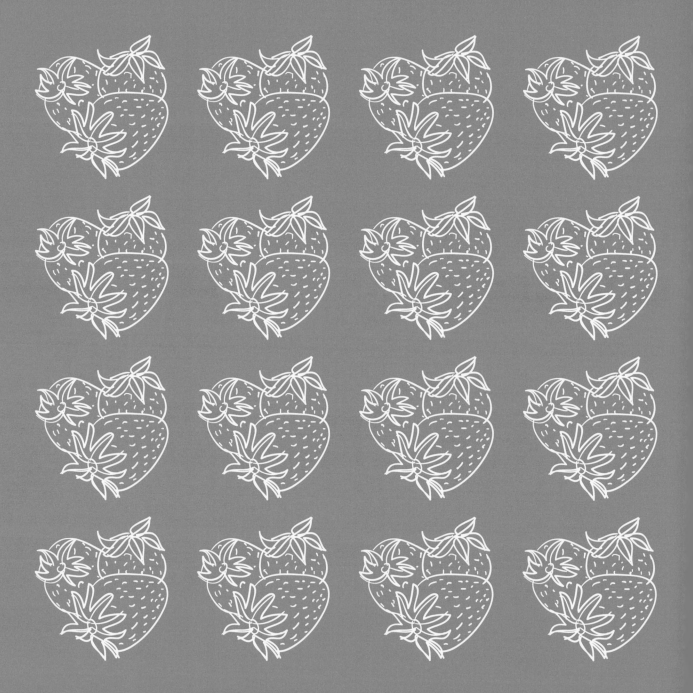

The first thing to do in this chapter is to explain the difference between a food allergy and a food intolerance:

FOOD ALLERGY *

When someone has an allergic reaction to a food it means that something in that particular food or drink triggers a response from the immune system. It is possible, though relatively rare, that if the reaction is severe it can be fatal.

An allergic reaction to a food or drink tends to happen within minutes of eating or drinking the offending substance although, in some cases, it can be up to several hours. It is possible for a doctor to test for a food allergy using an allergen-specific IgE blood test, a RAST blood test or skin-prick IgE test. If you want to have your child tested for a food allergy, always go to a medically qualified doctor and do not opt for alternative therapy-style testing (such as kinesiology, hair analysis, MAST tests, IgG blood tests, cytotoxic tests, pulse tests and Vega tests). These sorts of tests should not be used because they do not have good clinical evidence to prove their effectiveness or reliability and could give you false-positive or false-negative results. The former put you to a lot of unnecessary stress and work, eliminating foods unnecessarily; the latter could be fatal.

If you think that your baby has a food allergy, go to your GP. They can refer you to an allergy specialist.

FOOD INTOLERANCE

When someone has an intolerance to a food or drink, they will also experience certain unpleasant symptoms after eating or drinking it but, in this case, they are usually linked with an inability to digest a food properly (such as the sugar lactose in milk, for example, which leads to symptoms like diarrhoea or vomiting). The immune system is not involved in the response and it is generally not life-threatening. In most cases, symptoms usually occur several hours, or even longer, after the food or drink is consumed.

The only way to test properly for an intolerance to a food or drink is to exclude the substance in a controlled way with the help of a qualified Registered Dietitian or your GP.

HOW MANY BABIES ARE AFFECTED BY FOOD ALLERGIES?

These days, it does seem that more people than ever suffer with allergic reactions to foods but, in reality, there are no accurate figures to enable us to pinpoint exact numbers. According to the British Dietetic Association, between 6 and 8 per cent of children suffer and around 3 per cent of adults (although approximately 20 per cent of grown-ups think they have a food allergy).

WHICH FOODS ARE MOST LIKELY TO CAUSE ALLERGIC REACTIONS?

In practice, the foods to which children are most likely to have an allergic reaction include eggs, peanuts, milk, soya, nuts in general and wheat (although allergies to 'new' foods like kiwi and sesame seeds are becoming more commonplace).

Children less than three are more prone to developing allergic reactions to foods than grown-ups but the good news is that it is quite common for babies and toddlers to grow out of them as they move into childhood. Those with allergies to peanuts, nuts and shellfish, however, often do not and these allergies can remain dangerous, or even life-threatening, for life.

According to the Food Standards Association (before its nutrition section was moved, recently, to the Department of Health): in addition to peanuts, eggs, milk, fish, shellfish, wheat and soya, another seven types of foods account for 90 per cent of all allergic reactions to food in the UK. These are celery, other cereals containing gluten (such as rye, barley and oats), lupin, mustard, sesame seeds and foods or drinks containing the preservatives sulphur dioxide or sulphites (found in soft drinks, for example, and on dried fruit). Other less common food triggers are kiwi, coconut, fruit and vegetables generally, meat, pine nuts, rice, spices and vegetable oils.

HOW DO I KNOW IF MY BABY IS HAVING AN ALLERGIC REACTION?

Things to look for in babies are: a rash and itchy skin; swollen lips (and throat, although this is hard to tell in a baby); shortness of breath and wheezing; coughing; diarrhoea and/or vomiting; itchy, red and sore eyes; and a blocked or runny nose. If you think that your baby or child has reacted to a food or drink with any of these symptoms you should seek medical help urgently. It can be hard to tell the difference between a normal runny nose and one linked to an allergic reaction but it is vital to be safe rather than sorry. If you are unsure, get medical help as quickly as possible.

HOW LIKELY IS IT THAT MY BABY WILL HAVE A FOOD ALLERGY?

No-one can predict for sure whether a baby is going to suffer with a food allergy or experience an intolerance to a food or drink. If either you or close family members have a food allergy or are prone to asthma, eczema, hayfever or any other type of allergies (to cat fur, house dust and so on) or if your baby has eczema, then there is a chance that they may be more prone to developing food allergies. You must discuss this with your health visitor and GP.

If your baby is diagnosed with a food allergy it is important to try to continue breastfeeding (or, if not, bottle feeding with formula advised by your GP or health visitor) until she or he is six months of age.

As mentioned, the foods most likely to trigger allergy (including peanuts, eggs, cows' milk, nuts, seeds, wheat, fish and shellfish) should not be introduced before six months. When they are, they should be given separately in a very small quantity so that any reaction can be carefully monitored. If any reaction does begin, medical advice should be sought urgently.

Trust your own instincts and if you are at all worried or have the slightest hunch about a food, avoid it for as long as possible. I had a strange feeling about my son, Freddie, and eggs. My own mother had told me I'd had a bad reaction to them when I was six months old and although I hadn't felt they would be a problem with my daughter, I had a sixth sense about Freddie. One day we were having lunch in Italy and a friend leaned over and gave him some omelette. My son was ten months old. Within minutes, he was scratching madly and came out in an all-over rash and his mouth began to swell up. It was extremely scary. I whipped him directly to hospital where he was given medication to bring the swelling under control. Everything began to subside but, as you can imagine, I have not let him have eggs since. Now I have to carry an adrenalin shot with me and anti-histamine medication at all times just in case any egg slips through the net.

Peanut allergy

Peanut allergy needs a section of its own. Again, if a member of your close family has any kind of allergy or eczema there is an increased chance of your baby having a peanut allergy. Speak with your health visitor or GP before giving any kind of peanut-containing food for the first time and never give any form of peanut before six months of age.

Allergy to cows' milk

Some babies are born with an allergy to the protein in cows' milk. Given that the proteins in sheep and goats' milks are very similar to those in cows' milk, it is likely that if your baby is allergic to the latter they will be to the former, and possibly to soya milk as well. Again, talk this through with your health visitor and GP and follow their advice. It is possible that your GP may prescribe a special infant formula, in which the protein has been altered to make it acceptable, which your baby will be able to tolerate.

Allergy to cows' milk protein is totally different to an intolerance to the sugar in cows' milk, called lactose, which is due to having too little of the enzyme called lactase. A child may grow out of cows' milk allergy and they may be able to tolerate small amounts of dairy foods, in spite of the lactose intolerance, as they grow older. Everyone is different so each child needs to be treated as an individual case.

WHAT IS AN ANAPHYLACTIC REACTION?

This is when several symptoms of allergic reaction occur at the same time. For example, a person's lips can swell, their throat can close up, their blood pressure can fall, they can develop a rash, and can lose consciousness – all at once. Not surprisingly, this is very serious and, unless treated immediately, can be fatal. It is treated by injecting adrenaline, a hormone that jolts the system back into action. It is vital that people diagnosed with food allergies carry adrenalin injections with them at all times and, in the case of infants, toddlers and children, people caring for them should carry them and know when and how to administer. Peanuts, milk, eggs and fish are the most common foods to trigger anaphylactic shock.

HOW TO AVOID ALLERGY TRIGGER FOODS

Obviously you need to avoid the 'whole' food concerned, such as eggs, milk, peanuts or shellfish, but when buying pre-packaged foods these may be included as ingredients. It is vital that you check the ingredients list of any packaged food you buy VERY carefully. You need to do this every time you select a particular item because manufacturers can alter recipes so that ingredients can change from one purchase to another.

Some foods have information about which potential allergens are in their products. My advice is always check the ingredients list anyway. It is the only surefire way of knowing whether a food is present. You will notice that some foods carry a warning such as 'may contain nuts' or 'may contain milk'. This means that, even though these ingredients are not present in the food itself and do not appear on the food label or ingredients list, they have been produced in a factory where the offending allergen may have cross-contaminated the product.

Eating away from home

If eating out, I would always recommend taking food with you if your child has a severe food allergy. I just wouldn't trust any establishment with my child's health.

Intolerance to milk sugar

An intolerance to lactose, the sugar in milk, is very rare in babies but if it does occur it is due to a baby's digestive system being unable to make enough of the enzyme lactase, which breaks down lactose in our bodies. This is not an allergy but can lead to bloating, tummy cramps, diarrhoea and lots of unhappy crying. Usually, if a baby is intolerant to lactose it cannot cope with cows', sheep or goats' milk sugar either. It will need a special formula from birth onwards and, once weaned, will need to be given lactose-free milk alternatives like soya milk fortified with calcium and vitamins.

Intolerance to fruit sugar

Some babies and children may be intolerant to fructose, a fruit sugar found in virtually all fruits as well as in many foods (including some baby foods) where it is used as a sweetener. Fructose is also found in sucrose (sugar) as sucrose is made up of one molecule of glucose and one of fructose. The intolerance occurs when a person lacks the enzyme aldose B, which is needed to break down fructose in the digestive system. It is an inherited condition so you are likely to be aware that your baby may be affected. It is estimated that up to one in 20,000 people may have fructose intolerance in some European countries.

A baby can experience various symptoms from convulsions to extreme tiredness, looking yellow and jaundiced (being unable to digest fructose leads to metabolites that affect the liver), being off their food and vomiting (especially after eating fructose or sucrose). If you suspect your baby may be affected it is very important to see your GP and get an appointment with a Registered Dietitian to help you plan a well-balanced diet without these sugars.

HOW CAN I ENSURE THAT MY CHILD HAS A GOOD DIET IF ALLERGIC OR INTOLERANT TO CERTAIN FOODS?

My advice is to ask your GP to refer you to an allergy specialist who works with a Registered Dietitian with an expertise in this area. They will be able to help you plan a nutritious and interesting diet for your little one while pointing out the potential pitfalls. The idea is to build up a repertoire of foods and drinks that fulfil all your child's nutritional needs to ensure that they grow and develop optimally. We all need a well-balanced selection of foods in our diets that we enjoy and children with food allergies or intolerances are no exception.

Never just chop out a whole food group, such as dairy foods, under your own steam because you suspect that you child may have an intolerance to them. Get the right professional advice and then, if diagnosed, work your way around the excluded foods so that you have a diet that is doable and enjoyable, fitting in with your family budget and general eating habits. Always talk with your GP about food allergies and intolerances because some products that will help you to cope are available on prescription.

FOOD ADDITIVES

Food contains additives for a variety of reasons. They are used to prevent food poisoning, to stop food going off, and to provide colour, flavour or texture. Some food additives are natural substances and some are synthetic. Any additives put into food must, by law, be shown on the label. Additives with an 'E' number have been tested and passed as safe for use in EU countries.

Some children (and some adults) have adverse reactions to certain food additives, hyperactive behaviour being the most common. A diet high in processed foods is not only more likely to contain additives but it will probably be high in salt, sugar and fat. For this reason alone, these foods are worth avoiding. Try and replace processed foods with fresh 'whole' foods like lean meat, chicken, fish, nuts, seeds, pulses, fruits, vegetables and starchy foods. You will cut down on fats, sugars and additives while upping your vitamins, minerals, super-nutrients and general quality of diet.

Chapter Five

Organic – Is It Worth It?

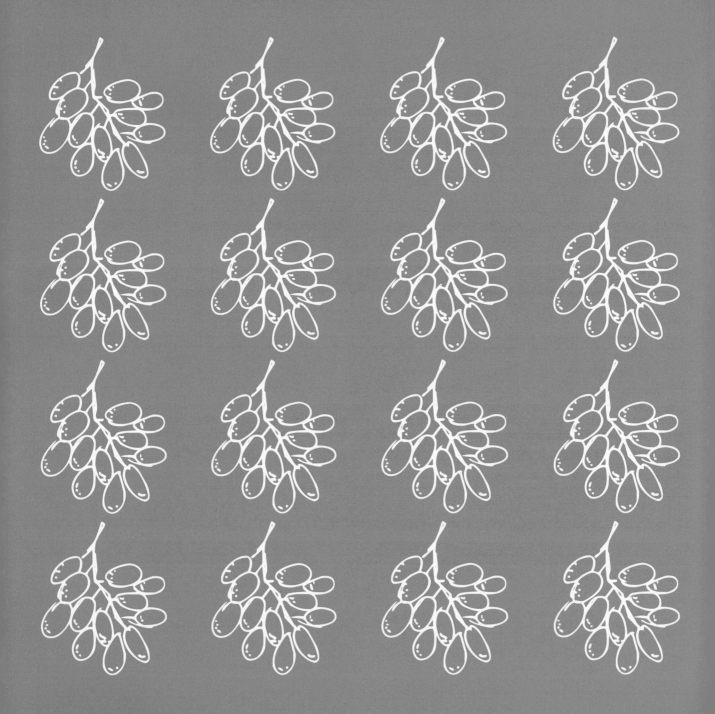

ORGANIC *

Putting aside the very important view that organic farming methods are believed to be better for the environment, and therefore our planet, many mums want to know whether organic food is actually 'better' for their children. This is a tricky one because while instinctively and intuitively I feel that it simply has to be, there are arguments for both organic and conventional farming methods. The bottom line is that conventionally produced food has to meet many strict safety criteria to be allowed on our shelves and this is especially true of baby foods.

I hope that the information in this chapter, organised in a question and answer format, helps you to make up your own mind as to where you lie in this famously difficult-to-decide area of life. When I get tied in knots about the issue, I often sit and think that in many countries people do not have the luxury of this choice. Lots and lots of people don't, and it's probably worth bearing this in mind. It adds another perspective.

ARE ORGANIC MEAT, POULTRY, MILK AND EGGS HEALTHIER THAN NON-ORGANIC?

The routine use of antibiotics found in standard farming practice to suppress disease and act as growth promoters is banned in organic farms. In practice, they are not needed as much due to the extra space organic animals and poultry are allocated and their free-range lifestyles, making the risk of a disease outbreak much reduced. If antibiotics are used to treat a problem in organic farming there are strict minimum time limits set for when an animal may be milked or slaughtered to prevent any residues of antibiotics being found in their milk or meat.

In conventional farming, veterinary medicines are given to animals if they are poorly. These can include vaccines and antibiotics, medicines for infected skin and hooves, anti-flea and worm treatments and sheep dips. Small residual quantities of such medicines, including steroid hormones and additives added to animal feed, can get into our meat and poultry. However, where they do, the Food Standards Agency in the UK says they are usually at very low levels and, to make sure that food is safe to eat, many medicines have a specific amount of withdrawal time that must pass before treated animals can be slaughtered for their meat or other products, such as milk and eggs. The FSA also assures us that acceptable maximum residue levels are set and strictly adhered to, with regular Government checks carried out to ensure that levels present in the food are safe. Apparently, they almost always are. If not, they are taken off the market.

It's your choice whether you buy organic meat and poultry. In all honesty, if you want to lower the chances of your child consuming residues of drugs and additives you are probably best off going for organic. If, on the other hand, you accept that levels of these substances in conventional produce are safe for humans, as we are told by the FSA, then you will probably feel confident going for these. Anyway, our choices will be affected by the cost and availability of various alternatives.

ARE ORGANIC FRUITS, VEGETABLES AND CEREALS BETTER THAN NON-ORGANIC?

Buying organic food is a way of minimising the amount of pesticide residues on the food we eat. Organic farmers usually avoid using them and the very few that are allowed are only permitted on a small number of crops. Pesticides are used in conventional farming to prevent diseases in crops, kill off pests like mice and insects, control weeds and help to stop them going mouldy when stored.

At the moment there is only a small amount of evidence linking pesticides eaten in our diet with health problems in humans. We do not really know what are the potential toxic effects from eating pesticide residues over a lifetime or the effect of different pesticide residues combining to give a cocktail-effect within our bodies but if you want to reduce pesticide consumption, then go for organic food. This said, the health benefits of eating standard fruit and vegetables are immense and the risk of eliminating them, we are told, far outweighs the risks posed by possible exposure to pesticide residues. Washing fruits and vegetables can lower some residue levels while peeling others like carrots and parsnips can have a similar effect.

As with levels of veterinary medicine residues in animal products like meat and chicken, levels of pesticide residues in conventionally farmed fruits, vegetables and cereals are monitored. They are also monitored in meat, fish and dairy products (given that animals eat these foods), as well as in processed foods – including baby foods – to ensure that they are within legal and safe limits. Obviously the idea that pesticide residues may be found in baby foods is not appealing. As with any other processed foods, levels are monitored and, because the area is so sensitive, anyone who makes baby foods goes to huge lengths to keep them to an absolute minimum. Those that have been found, the authorities tell us, are at levels low enough not to be dangerous to an infant's health.

ARE ORGANIC FOODS BETTER FOR YOU NUTRITIONALLY?

From a nutritional point of view it would make sense that a chicken that has been allowed to run around outside has, for example, better-developed muscles in its legs and therefore more of the mineral iron (which is needed to transport oxygen to exercising muscles) in its leg meat. Equally, it would make sense that a tomato that is grown under natural, rather than artificial, sunlight develops more of the colourful red pigments, such as lycopene, used to protect itself from sun damage (and which is believed to have health benefits for humans). However, one of the most recent reviews of the nutritional differences between organic and non-organic foods has concluded that while differences have been found, they are not 'important'. This infuriated many organic supporters who say that any difference is still significant in terms of nutritional wellbeing and that well-designed studies now need to be conducted to make proper comparisons.

The Soil Association points out that protein-rich foods did have more protein in some organic versions and there was more of the immune-boosting mineral zinc. The study also revealed higher levels of the potentially heart-friendly super-nutrients, known as flavonoids, in fruits and vegetables and 54 per cent more of the orange antioxidant pigment beta carotene, believed to help to protect our eyes and skin from sun damage. Levels of other nutrients such as copper, needed for good skin pigmentation, magnesium for good muscle function, phosphorus for strong bones and potassium for blood pressure control were also up in organic compared to conventionally-produced food. The study also revealed that there were higher levels of polyunsaturated fats in organic meat and dairy foods. (It has been well-documented, in the past, that organic milk has higher levels of omega 3 essential fats and organic fruit and vegetables can have much, much more vitamin C.)

I know many mums who prefer to use fewer animal products in their diets and when they do, opt for organic versions. Equally, I know others who are well-informed and feel safe with standard meat, chicken, fish, eggs and milk. As with the research findings, opinion is very much divided and you should choose what makes you feel comfortable. The one area in which I do make an effort to buy organic when I can is milk. We use a lot of it in our house and, if there were any residues of medicines or pesticides, we would be getting a fair bit due to the sheer quantity consumed. It's just a hunch.

WHAT ABOUT BSE?

The Soil Association banned the feeding of animal protein to ruminants (like cows) in 1983, five years before the government took action to do so in conventional farming. Soil Association standards ban any animal not born and reared on an organic farm being sold as organic beef and they have found no cases of BSE in any animal born and reared organically.

DO ORGANIC PROCESSED FOODS CONTAIN FOOD ADDITIVES?

A wide range and large quantity of additives are used in conventional food processing. Only 30 are allowed in organic food and drink products and they are only permitted if the producer can prove that their product really cannot be made or preserved without them. Substances banned for use include: hydrogenated fats; phosphoric acid (found in cola); the sweetener, aspartame; the flavour-enhancer, monosodium glutamate; and sulphur dioxide, used in fruit juices, soft drinks, wine, beer, sauces and on dried fruit. (Sulphur dioxide is, however, allowed in organic wine but the levels permitted are a third of those in non-organic wine.)

The fact is, if you opt for an organic version of biscuits, cakes, bread, lemonade or ready-meals, they are almost certainly going to contain fewer additives than conventional products (and none that have been associated with negative health reactions), although they will have similar calorie, fat, sugar and salt levels.

DOES ORGANIC FOOD TASTE BETTER?

Sometimes but not always. Organic meat and poultry are usually more flavourful and I do really notice a taste difference in our locally reared organic chicken. Vegetables and fruits tend to depend on the type of seed used. As with lycopene levels, again it makes sense, however, that a tomato allowed to ripen in the sun, growing at its own natural speed over many weeks in nutrient-rich soil, is going to be a lot tastier than one produced hyperponically at breakneck speed in a greenhouse.

But, then again, there are tomatoes grown non-organically outside, which can taste great too. We have a local grower, close to where I live, who produces truly delicious non-organic tomatoes. I guess you need to taste and see.

THE SIX MILLION DOLLAR QUESTION: ARE ORGANIC WEANING AND INFANT FOODS BETTER?

There are very strict laws in place for the production of all infant and baby food (a category that legally spans from first weaning foods to three years of age).

I think you need to use the information above to work out how you feel about the infant food category. Given that it is generally best to make your own weaning purées and to introduce your children to family meals, these products should be used as back-up rather than being relied on as a sole source of nutrition. If this is the case, you could say on the one hand, a small amount of conventional products can't do any harm. On the other, if you are only using them occasionally, you may feel organic is worth the extra cost.

Chapter Six

When Shortcuts Are a Must

Most baby food in bottles, jars and pouches (organic, standard or otherwise), which is found on supermarket shelves next to the rusks and cotton wool, has a shelf life of around 18 months, which, in theory, means that the pouch of lamb hot-pot or apricot pudding you give your nine-month-old could have been produced at the time they were being conceived.

Of course such foods are perfectly safe because all ambient baby foods have to be heat treated to 121°C for a minimum of at least four minutes to kill any bugs present in the ingredients. It is this process that gives them such a long shelf life. However, this processing almost wholly destroys vitamin C and most B vitamins, dulls the natural pigments in foods, making the end product less vibrant and colourful to look at, and alters the consistency and flavour of the original ingredients.

For me it was therefore a relief to discover a range of frozen infant purées and toddler ready-meals called Babylicious and Kiddylicious, created by a lady named Sally Preston. A food scientist by training and herself a mum of two little ones, she decided that she wanted to create another, altogether fresher, option for mothers to opt for. As Sally says: 'The science behind food and importance of flavour has always interested me. Once my children Hannah and Jack were born, I naturally wanted to feed them the best meals I could.' But also like many mums, there were times when she simply did not have the chance to whip up fresh meals. It gave her the idea to develop her ranges, which now also include frozen fruit yoghurts and fruit snacks.

The advantage of frozen meals is that the freezing process is the most natural way of preserving food. It does not require heat treatment and locks in the nutrients in the food so that levels are virtually the same once heated as in a home-cooked meal. Importantly for me, with frozen meals the colours and textures as well as the taste of the meals are as close as possible to home cooking, which is important when trying to get infants and toddlers to appreciate 'real' food. She hit the spot as far as I'm concerned and there are days when perhaps I've been working for the day away from the house, or am simply too shattered to rustle up a meal, when both Coco and Freddie have had one of her purées and as they grew older, one of her meals. On the whole, they seemed to enjoy them.

Although a fresh, balanced, home-cooked meal is in most cases the gold standard of infant or toddler feeding, because apart from anything to do with nutrition, making dinner for your children is an act of love and gets them used to seeing you cooking, something they will hopefully soon join in with, it is my view that both fresh and ambient products can have a role to play within a baby's or toddler's meal-time repertoire. Using them day in and day out, meal in and meal out, is absolutely not what I recommend, but when your situation or time scale dictates, they can be life-savers.

A BRIEF ROUND-UP OF SOME OF THE BEST ON THE MARKET (IN MY VIEW) *

FROZEN INFANT AND TODDLER MEALS

Make sure that you transport these products quickly from the supermarket to home and that your home freezer is working optimally. Using frozen meals means that when you come to heat them up you are probably actually serving up the most nutritionally favourable alternative to home cooking currently available on the market.

Babylicious and Kiddylicious

Babylicious is a range of weaning options such as Carrot, Parsnip and Potato Purée and Kiddylicious toddler meals like Spaghetti Bolognese. They contain no added salt or sugar and look and taste good. At the time of going to print, you could buy these meals direct from www.babylicious.co.uk or via Ocado.

BabyDeli

Another range of frozen weaning foods but this time made from organic ingredients which are handmade into purées and can be microwaved from frozen. The range includes organic Cauliflower Purée (which comes in trays of ten frozen cubes) along with for example, frozen pear and plum purées. At the last look, they were available from Ocado and www.kitchenmonkey.co.uk.

FRESH BABY AND TODDLER MEALS

Little Dish

This used to be a 'fresh' range of infant and toddler meals with just a five-day shelf life in the chill cabinet of supermarkets. Unfortunately, they have now gone down the route of heat treating the meals to extend their shelf life to two weeks plus. This sadly affects nutrients, lowering levels of B and C vitamins, and affects the way they look, taste and feel in the mouth.

They do, however, still boast no added salt and sugar.

Available from Tesco, Sainsbury's, Waitrose and Ocado.

Annabel Karmel

The Annabel Karmel range includes Annabel Karmel's Eat Fussy meals, which include sauces for weaning and 'fresh' ready-meals for toddlers. These do contain some added salt and sugar and have, unlike the Little Dish range, been pasteurised to allow a longer shelf life in the chill cabinet of two weeks plus. The pasteurisation process will lead to loss of heat-soluble vitamins, like C and

B vitamins, and the fact that the meals are OK to eat two weeks or more from the time of production in itself will lead to further losses of such nutrients along with, probably, some of the vibrancy in how they look and taste compared with a fresh home-cooked meal. In this range you can expect to find dishes for toddlers like Salmon and Cod Pie, Chicken with Rice and Vegetable Pasta Bakes.

Available from Sainsbury's.

AMBIENT BABY AND TODDLER FOODS

Recent research from the University of Bristol reveals how a poor diet at age three and below has a significant impact on long-term performance in school, regardless of subsequent changes of diet in later life. If you have time to make a fresh, home-prepared purée or toddler meal and compare your dish with ambient versions it is easy to discern the difference in taste and colour. The concern is that if babies are fed very regularly on the ambient versions it is conceivable that their taste buds may be less happy to accept a normal, healthy diet post-weaning.

This is not to say that ambient baby food has no place in infant and toddler nutrition. The processing does not affect the amount of nutrients like protein, minerals (such as iron), or many of the super-nutrient antioxidant pigments (like the orange beta carotene in carrots or the red lycopene in tomatoes). In fact, when it comes to the latter the pigments can be digested more easily than if they were eaten raw as a result of the heat treatment (or home cooking methods) they have undergone.

The other obvious thing in ambient meals' favour is the convenience factor. Having travelled to and from Italy with my children as babies, the Plum brand of ambient weaning foods came into its own as the meals come in convenient and lightweight plastic pots. They were an essential part of my hand luggage, helping to keep Freddie well fed en route when chilled fresh versions were not an option. I also always had a couple packed in my bag for those 'just-in-case' moments when we wanted to spend an extra hour at the beach or in the park instead of having to race home to get supper prepared.

Here is a selection of some on the market:

Plum baby foods

Plum has a range of organic ambient purées for all stages of weaning, which includes Blueberry, Banana and Vanilla plus meals for the over-ones, such as Giant Couscous with Chicken, and Squash and Sweet Potato. As mentioned above, the plastic tubs in which Plum meals are packaged make this range particularly lightweight and portable and, although ambient products, their flavours are good.

Available in all good supermarkets.

Ella's Kitchen

Another highly portable organic range, these weaning products come in a pouch, which can be squeezed directly onto a spoon, making them really good news if travelling on a plane or train as you get no spillage. Meals for babies include apple and banana purée while at ten months they can tuck into dishes like Comforting Cottage Pie. The only problem I have with this range is that you cannot see what is in the pouch; I prefer a toddler meal to be in a pot or jar where the food is visible.

Available from the larger supermarkets.

Hipp Organic

An ambient product, which comes in jars. The advantage is that you can see the colour and texture of the food inside so at least you do know what you are getting. The range includes meals like Tender Carrots and Potato. The disadvantage is that the glass jars make them heavier to carry around and I worry slightly about them breaking with children about.

Available from all good supermarkets and some pharmacies.

Organix

Another organic range in a jar, the plus and minus points for the brand are very similar to Hipp Organic. Meals like Vegetables with Chicken and Wholegrain Rice do not look too bad and taste OK.

Available from all good supermarkets and some pharmacies.

It may seem counter-intuitive, but while heat-sensitive vitamins, like vitamin C and many B vitamins, are damaged and diminished through heat and cooking processes that involve water, such as boiling, minerals, protein and many super-nutrients are not.

In the case of pigments like the red lycopene in tomatoes and the orange beta carotene in carrots, they are actually better absorbed once the food is cooked. This is because cooking helps to break down cell walls and allow the pigments to be released and be more easily absorbed by the gut. They are also more easily absorbed in the presence of fat because they are soluble in fat. Thus, tomatoes made into a Bolognese sauce are particularly good and easily absorbed sources of lycopene. So too are carrots, cooked and served with a little olive oil.

Raw tomatoes and carrots are also nutritious, but the good news is that cooked ones are certainly not nutritionally inferior.

With vegetables like broccoli and spinach, cooking makes pigments like lutein (which is yellow but is hidden by the stronger, green pigments) and beta carotene more available but slightly lowers the level of vitamin C. The shorter the cooking time and the less water used in the cooking process, the less vitamin C is lost. That is why steaming and microwaving are good ways of preserving the heat- and water-soluble nutrients while enhancing absorption of the super-nutrient pigments.

Chapter Seven

Mum's Nutrition

Of course it is really important to ensure that you try to feed your baby the best possible food. It shapes their future health in so many ways and affects their inherent likes and dislikes. However, how many of us consider our own nutritional needs after our baby is born? We may put a lot of effort into eating the right diet to improve our chances of falling pregnant and we may think about what we eat while breastfeeding but how many of us continue this kind of self-care once we get past these stages?

Speaking from experience and from chatting with mums, the thing we all notice is that in our quest to provide the best food we can for our children, somehow our own needs begin to slip off the radar. And this happens just as our bodies are trying to cope with the cumulative effect of having:

1.   **Created a whole new person (with the drain this has on our own nutritional reserves).**

2.   **Broken nights. (A lack of sleep can affect everything from your immune function to your ability to concentrate and think rationally and it can definitely affect your mood!)**

3.   **The need to juggle modern lives, which can include going back to work.**

Not looking after ourselves is a problem not just because poor nutrition depletes our already tired bodies, leaving us even more worn-out and susceptible to mild or full-blown depression, but it leaves our bodies in a bad place for a future pregnancy, should we want it.

GETTING A GOOD NIGHT'S SLEEP *

Re-establishing good sleeping habits after you have become used to jumping out of bed to tend to feeds, nappy changes or just to check on a baby can be hard. So when you do have the chance of a clear run at a whole night of sleep you really want to make the most of it. What and when you eat and drink may have a role to play in helping to do just that.

With the exception of food and drinks containing caffeine or too much alcohol, research in the area of how food affects sleep is not terribly conclusive. Anecdotally, however, some foods do seem to make falling and staying asleep harder, while others appear to help you nod off and have a peaceful night.

DEFINITE SLEEP DISRUPTORS *

CAFFEINE

We all know that caffeine stimulates our nervous system and helps to keep us awake. Sensible advice is to avoid drinking at bedtime: coffee; tea; rich hot chocolate; and even some cold-remedy drinks (check the ingredients before taking). The important thing to remember, however, is the length of time caffeine takes to break down in our bodies and the speed with which this happens varies widely between people. Avoiding caffeine for two to three hours before bed may be sufficient to clear it from one person's system but for others it can take up to eight hours. In this case, they would need to avoid caffeine-containing drinks from the early afternoon onwards if they want to promote good sleep.

Amounts of caffeine in drinks:

Small 150ml cup of coffee	115mg of caffeine
Small 150ml cup of tea (average strength)	40mg
Small 150ml cup of tea (strong brew)	60mg
Mug (200ml) green or white tea	14mg to 61mg
Mug (200ml) decaffeinated tea	3mg to 6mg (can be less)
Can (330ml) regular or diet cola	36mg
Can (250ml) regular energy drink	150mg

Also take care to check the small print of cold remedies and painkillers. Some manufacturers add caffeine to perk you up, with some providing up to 60mg per serving or couple of tablets. It is also worth remembering that a 50g bar of dark chocolate can provide 40mg of caffeine along with other potentially stimulating compounds. Stick with a small section of dark chocolate or switch to milk chocolate with 10mg of caffeine per 50g. However, if you are sensitive to caffeine, it is probably best to avoid either at bedtime.

Something that came as a complete surprise to me was the news that some coffee ice creams also provide caffeine. I assumed that they just contained coffee flavouring but some luxury brands use real coffee, which could add 58mg of caffeine to your daily intake from an average-sized serving.

ALCOHOL

Unfortunately, while an alcoholic drink can help you fall asleep it can then disrupt the really beneficial 'restorative' sleep later in the night. It is best to avoid alcohol before bed.

LIKELY SLEEP DISRUPTORS *

GINGER/GINSENG

Herbalists refer to ginger as a 'stimulating' herb so it may well be worth avoiding ginger tea infusions, ginger beer, ginger biscuits and so on prior to bedtime. Ginseng is another herb to avoid because, while it is said to help to boost energy, high doses have been linked with insomnia.

CHEESE

People often say that cheese keeps them awake or gives them bad dreams. Little evidence supports its sleep-depriving properties although its high fat content means it can sit in the stomach causing indigestion and restlessness. The same is true of any fat-rich meal so the advice for evening eating is to keep it light.

MALTED DRINKS

Oddly enough, it may also be worth trying to avoid malted drinks. Although they are specifically marketed for 'bedtime', many give you up to four teaspoons of sugar, which can raise your blood sugar rather quickly, make you feel slightly buzzy.

LIKELY SLEEP INDUCERS *

While certain foods and drinks disrupt sleep, others appear to help to lull you into it, keeping you sleeping through the night.

MILKY DRINK

A milky drink at bedtime is certainly worth a try. Milk contains the protein building-block tryptophan, an amino acid that enhances sleep. However, one cup would not contain enough to have this effect, which means that its soothing benefits may simply be psychological. But if it works for you, it works.

RICE FOR DINNER

A carbohydrate-rich dinner may also help. Carbohydrates are said to help in the production of the feel-good, destressing brain chemical, serotonin. Something like a filled baked potato or a tomato pasta dish would fit the bill. In Australia, scientists showed that people who ate a bowl of rice before bedtime slept well, probably because it helped to release serotonin.

REGULAR MEAL PATTERNS

Some sleep experts say that people who eat at regular times throughout the day usually have more regular sleep habits. Since this is a good habit to get into anyway, this is certainly a pattern worth adopting.

CHAMOMILE TEA

It is an old remedy and a good one because chamomile contains plant compounds, which have similar effects on areas of brains as anti-anxiety drugs do in helping us relax. Chamomile can help us de-stress, fall asleep and stay asleep.

WHAT TO EAT AFTER A BAD NIGHT'S SLEEP *

I am writing this after a horrendous night with my children waking so many times that I lost count. I simply got up, zombie-like, to sort out whatever the problems were, each time falling back into a fitful sleep, made worse because the air-conditioning where we are staying kept switching itself off and on and waking me every time in the process.

What did I feel like eating once it was time to get up? As much sugar-rich 'stuff' that I could lay my hands on. A poor night's sleep does genuinely mess up your hormones the following morning, lowering levels of leptin while increasing insulin. Both trigger cravings for fast-release carbohydrate, such as toast with lashings of marmalade, sugary cereals and croissants, which only serve to make you feel sluggish yet craving more. I imagine our bodies crave these kinds of foods because after eating them we tend to feel sleepy and want to lay down to rest. Of course, when you are a mum you don't have this luxury and these fast-release carbohydrate foods only compound the problem because you have to keep going.

This morning, I could happily have eaten a whole box of Crunchy Nut Cornflakes but somehow I dragged myself to the fridge and put a couple of eggs on to boil. Ultimately, if you give in to your body's desire for a sugar-hit you risk jumping onto a sugar rollercoaster for the rest of the day, craving a sugar top-up every time your body manages to clear the previous lot from your bloodstream. A couple of eggs with some wholemeal toast, on the other hand, balance blood sugars and keep you feeling full, making the desire for sugary foods magically subside. I'm happy to say it worked for me: I've managed to write this part of the book and will get back to being a mum once the children wake from their morning sleep.

My advice is, when you have one bad night or many broken nights on the trot, try really hard to resist the sugar-craving. Instead, go for something nutritious and sustaining to get you through the morning ahead.

For a sustaining breakfast, try one of these:

- **a lean bacon sandwich; a milky coffee with one spoonful of sugar (taken with the milk, it will give you a little energy lift without setting you off on a sugar rollercoaster)**

- a bowl of porridge with a little honey

- a couple of Oatibix with a banana

- a bowl of sugar-free muesli with a chopped apple

- a homemade smoothie using fat-free Greek yoghurt, a banana and any other fruit you have to hand. (Real Greek yoghurt – rather than 'Greek-style' yoghurt – is filling because of its higher protein content.)

All of the above are good blood-sugar balancing ways to start the day after a hopeless night of broken sleep.

While it is best to avoid coffee or tea at bedtime, limiting yourself to a couple of cups during the day, using them when you really need that energy lift, can be a really effective way of making this chemical work for you.

WHAT TO EAT WHEN YOUR GET UP AND GO HAS, JUST GENERALLY, GOT UP AND GONE *

My nana, who was 96 at the time, once said to me that her 'get up and go had got up and gone'. At that age, I think she had every reason to feel tired. Then, when I had Freddie, I suddenly understood what she meant. I went from being an energy-rich, leap-out-of-bed-and-face-the-day type of person to a drag-myself-upright incarnation. I think the one thing that kept me on track was my decision to eat energy-boosting foods and leave those that I knew depleted my energy for times when I had the reserves to deal with them.

EATING FOR ENERGY

Because food is turned into fuel, another word for energy, the types you choose seem to affect energy levels. A steady supply of slowly digested carbohydrates really help to keep you going in the hours after eating.

Slow-release carbohydrate foods include:

porridge oats
sugar-free muesli
tortilla wraps
pasta

basmati rice

plain boiled noodles

sweet potatoes

pitta/rye/sourdough/granary breads.

Trying to base your meals around these kinds of carbohydrates should not only help to ensure a gentle supply of energy but also have the advantage of being pretty filling. Try adding to them chicken or fish, dairy foods like milk and low-fat cheeses, or some lean red meats like beef or extra-lean lamb. Quorn, tofu and pulses are also good choices. These foods are all protein-rich and not only help to keep us feeling full but also boost our concentration and make us feel mentally 'alive'.

IRON – ARE YOU GETTING ENOUGH?

Around 40 per cent of women in the UK in their 20s and 30s, and probably plenty in their 40s too, do not hit the daily recommended target for the mineral iron. This is a potential problem because a lack of iron over a prolonged period can lead to full-blown anaemia, which must be treated by your doctor. In the meantime, it can lead to sub-clinical anaemia, which can leave you feeling washed out, stressed and barely able to put one foot in front of the other.

We need 14.8mg of iron a day. Let's call it 15mg to round it up. Take a look at a typical day's food below. You can see that, although day one seems pretty healthy: lots of fruit and vegetables, lean chicken and skimmed milk, it provides only just over half of our daily needs of iron. Day two, on the other hand, just scrapes in with the 15mg. The general trend for women to give up red meat hasn't helped this widespread problem.

DAY ONE – 1900 calories, 8mg iron

Breakfast: fruit salad and yoghurt, and skimmed milk cappuccino

Snack: banana and apple

Lunch: cottage cheese with baked potato and salad, plus a fromage frais

Snack: healthy cereal bar and fruit smoothie

Dinner: grilled chicken with noodles and vegetables

DAY TWO – 1900 calories, 15mg iron

Breakfast: two poached eggs on a slice of granary toast

Snack: 5 dried apricots with a handful (8) of cashew nuts

Lunch: canned crab in a light mayonnaise dressing in a wholemeal pitta with salad, followed by a yoghurt

Snack: oatcake with ricotta cheese

Dinner: beef stir-fry with noodles and vegetables

Best foods for iron

From animal foods:

Lean beef

Lean lamb

Sardines canned in tomato sauce

Anchovies

Kippers

Mackerel

Pilchards

Brown crab meat and canned crab

Pheasant

Venison

Tuna canned in oil

From vegetables and cereals:

Dark green vegetables

Cashew nuts

Sesame seeds

Sunflower seeds

Almonds

Brazil nuts and hazelnuts

Mixed nuts

Peanuts

Peanut butter

Tahini paste

Dried apricots

Dried figs

Fortified breakfast cereals like All Bran and Bran Flakes

Getting enough iron every day is hard. If you feel that it is too much to worry about right now, my advice is to take a daily multivitamin and mineral supplement. Look for one that has 50–75 per cent of the recommended daily allowance for all the nutrients it contains. Those with mega-doses are best avoided since too much of one vitamin or mineral can throw another out of balance and large doses can be dangerous.

OTHER THINGS TO WATCH FOR

Drinking enough

What and when we drink is another key factor in maximising the feelgood factor. Being dehydrated saps both physical and mental strength. You do not have to be wedded to a litre bottle of Evian or give up coffee to remain well hydrated. All fluids count towards your daily target of around one and a half litres a day. You will probably need more on hot days, days when you are extra energetic, when you are in heated environments and if you exercise or are continuing to breastfeed. This means that fruit juices, smoothies, coffees, teas, fizzy drinks, squashes and soups are all included in your daily fluid total. Of course, water is 'best', in as much as it is free from added colours, preservatives, sweeteners, caffeine and so on (although milk is good too if you are breastfeeding). However, it is good to know that fluids are fluids when it comes to hydration and that even tea and coffee are not the strong diuretics they were once thought to be, if drunk in moderation.

Replenishing your body for the 'next time round'

Hopefully, by now you will be inspired to eat differently to improve sleep and boost energy to get you through days of endless washing, looking after your little one and, of course, cooking healthy meals. And if you are thinking of trying for another baby, that is another really good reason to get your diet in hand so that your body is in good enough shape to sustain another pregnancy. In that way, a baby-to-be will be able to get the best it can from you while you, in turn, will survive another poten-tially nutrient-draining onslaught.

You will need enough of the nutrients listed below. Don't be too alarmed though: if you eat a well-balanced diet you should be getting what you need. The template for a healthy, balanced diet is to have the following food categories at each meal:

1. **Protein-rich foods, such as: lean meat; fish; lean chicken and turkey; milk and dairy foods; pulse vegetables including peas, lentils and chickpeas; Quorn; tofu or soya-based foods.**

2.   Slowly digested carbohydrates, such as: porridge; sugar-free muesli; pitta; pasta; tortilla wraps; plain noodles; new boiled potatoes and sweet potatoes.

3.   Plenty of fruits and vegetables.

Details on specific nutrients needed for conception and pregnancy

If trying to fall pregnant, stick with less than 200mg of caffeine a day and stop drinking alcohol. Next, take a look at the nutrients below and tick off mentally that you are eating the foods that contain them. You may feel, in addition to eating well, that a well-balanced multivitamin and mineral supplement with 50–75 per cent of our daily nutritional needs is worth taking. I did, and actually still do, to help build my stores back up post-pregnancy.

Folic acid

All women of childbearing age should be taking 400mcg (micrograms) of folic acid a day if there's even the slightest chance of them getting pregnant. Doing so reduces the risk of babies being born with the neural tube defect, spina bifida. If you are even vaguely contemplating having another baby and are not taking this supplement, go directly to the chemists, stock up and start taking it now.

We also need to get 200mcg from our food. The best ones for folic acid include:

fortified breakfast cereals (check the nutrition label); black-eyed beans; Brussels sprouts; peanuts and peanut butter; spinach; broccoli; chickpeas; avocados; oranges; baked beans; and wholegrain bread.

Quick note: when steaming and cooking vegetables, do so lightly because heat destroys folic acid.

Vitamin B1

We need this for energy. Some women fall below the recommended intake so, when planning your meals try to include things like yeast extract (such as Marmite), peas, oranges, fortified breakfast cereals, boiled potatoes, pork, wholegrain cereals (such as brown pasta), wholegrain bread, as well as eggs.

Vitamin B2

We need more of this vitamin when pregnant so get ahead of the game now. It is essential for good energy levels. We get pretty good slugs of B2 from dairy foods like milk (a pint of skimmed milk will cover your daily needs), along with yoghurt, fortified cereals, eggs, lean beef, chicken and yeast extract.

Vitamin B6

Your growing baby needs B6, another crucial pregnancy B vitamin. Although your own needs don't officially rise when pregnant, some women do not hit the 1.2mg daily target in the first place. It is therefore worth checking that you are eating some of the foods below regularly to make sure you get enough. Try to include cod, steamed salmon, canned tuna, turkey, beef, bananas, Brussels sprouts, cabbage, mangoes, avocados, fortified breakfast cereals and wheatgerm.

Vitamin C

This vitamin is important for healthy immunity, keeping our gums and skin in good condition as well as improving the absorption of iron from plant-based foods. Daily needs increase from 40mg to 50mg when pregnant. Most women get around 60mg a day, so should be OK, and if you are having your 'five a day' of fruits and vegetables you are probably getting more. All citrus fruits (like oranges and grapefruit), papaya, guava, blackcurrants and other berries, peppers, broccoli, kiwi fruit, cabbage and cauliflower are great for vitamin C.

Vitamin A

In the UK it is more of a worry that adults are getting too much, rather than not enough, vitamin A. Given that too much is a problem for your growing baby it is probably best, if you are thinking about having another baby, that you avoid vitamin A-rich fish-oil supplements.(This is why it is important not to supplement with any multivitamins that are not recommended by your doctor or have not been specifically designed for pregnant women.)

You get safe amounts of vitamin A from butter and margarine, eggs, whole milk and oily fish. Pregnant women should have no more than one serving of oily fish a week because of the pollutants they contain.

Vitamin D

We need this so-called sunshine vitamin to help our bodies absorb the bone-building mineral, calcium. Although, in theory, women should make enough vitamin D through the action of sunlight on our skin (which converts 'pro-vitamin D' into the active form) between the months of March and September in the UK, the fact remains that scientists think that many of us don't seem to manage this.

When pregnant, women need vitamin D from sunlight and 10 micrograms from their diet. There are few foods rich in this vitamin so most women may benefit from a 10mcg supplement daily to meet their needs. It is my view that you may as well start this process before falling pregnant – it can't do any harm. Meanwhile, you can get it in good amounts from oily fish like herrings, mackerel, sardines, trout and salmon but, remember, you are only supposed to have one serving a week when pregnant. Other foods with small amounts of vitamin D include margarine and eggs.

Magnesium

We all need magnesium for strong bones and teeth but also, importantly, this mineral is vital for supporting the very rapid division of cells that takes place just after conception. Research has revealed that poor intakes are associated with low birth weights. This can lead to complications like an increase in loss of infant life and/ or a risk of ill-health generally, including damage to the brain and nervous system.

The recommended intake each day for magnesium is 270mg. The reason we need to take particular care is because food surveys have revealed that, on average, women only seem to get around 237mg. This means that quite a lot of us need to increase our intake, especially when planning a pregnancy. You may as well start now by making sure that your diet includes wholegrain cereals (wholemeal and granary bread, rye crispbreads, wholegrain cereals etc.), sunflower and pumpkin seeds, nuts, peanut butter, pilchards, lentils and spinach.

Calcium

Calcium is vital to keep your own bones strong and, during pregnancy, to help in the development of your baby's bones. Unfortunately, your baby probably takes what it needs at your expense so it is doubly important that you protect your bones with enough calcium in your diet, especially after having one baby and planning another. Although the recommended intake is 700mg a day (whether you are pregnant or not), an average woman's intake in the UK, aged 16–34, falls below this. You don't want to start pregnancy lagging behind so it is well worth paying attention to your calcium intake right now.

We all know that you get lots of calcium in yoghurt and milk (skimmed is a little better than whole or semi-skimmed) but it is also found in fortified soya milks, steamed tofu, sesame seeds, sardines (canned and eaten with the bones – this can be your one portion of oily fish in the week), dried figs, green beans and other dark-green vegetables.

Zinc

Zinc is a mineral needed to help cells replicate, making it particularly important in the first weeks and months of pregnancy. If you start off with poor zinc reserves it could affect the development of your baby's brain and central nervous system. Women who are demi- or completely vegetarian can be low in zinc along with women who have taken the contraceptive pill for a long time and those who do a lot of hard fitness training. Target intakes are 7mg a day for all women, pregnant or not.

Eating a well-balanced diet should meet these needs but, to be sure, include foods like wheatgerm, pumpkin seeds, lean red meats (such as beef, lamb and pork) as well as canned crab and sardines canned in oil.

Iron

We need this mineral to oxygenate every cell in our bodies because iron helps to make the oxygen-carrying haemoglobin in our blood. During pregnancy, our iron needs do not increase, partly because we stop bleeding in menstruation and also because our bodies seem to switch on mechanisms designed to help us absorb more than usual.

As mentioned above (p.84), the problem is that around 40 per cent of women aged 18–34 in the UK do not get enough of this mineral in the first place. If you don't have enough during pregnancy, your body makes sure that the baby gets it by increasing the amount passing through the placenta. This can leave you feeling tired and stressed, having poor concentration and going down with infections more easily. If you develop full-blown iron-deficiency anaemia you could end up with a greater risk of your baby arriving early and being a low birthweight. It might even increase the risk of a baby not pulling through.

These are all good reasons for making sure that you eat foods such as lean red meats, oily fish like sardines, game meats like venison, and canned crab. Iron is well absorbed from these foods. You also get iron from plant foods such as dried apricots, fortified breakfast cereals, sesame seeds, cashew nuts and peanuts. Note that the tannin in tea reduces our ability to absorb iron from these foods while vitamin C-rich foods enhances it. In other words, avoid tea when having plant foods rich in iron and have a glass of orange juice or something rich in vitamin C, like peppers, with the meal instead.

You also need to think about your weight. Being underweight (having a Body Mass Index of less than 20) can lead to your periods stopping, which of course makes conception pretty much impossible. It is also associated with babies being born with a low birth weight – sometimes a reflection of a mother's diet being generally poor. Whatever the cause, it is a bad idea to be underweight when trying to have a baby.

A BMI of 23–24 seems to be optimal for fertility and your baby's ultimate birth weight. However, having a BMI of over 30 makes women less likely to conceive and if they do, they are at risk of encountering problems like raised blood pressure, pregnancy diabetes or pre-eclampsia, which can be dangerous to mum and baby. The best way to lose or gain weight is having a balanced diet, taking a daily vitamin and mineral supplement (with 50–70 per cent of the RDA of each included), and aiming to reach your target weight about two to three months before starting to try for a baby. If you are overweight, try and build in an hour of walking as many days as you can. If you are serious about getting pregnant and having a healthy pregnancy it is important you try and bring your BMI into the normal range. There is some information in the next section (p.98) if you want to find the best weight-loss plan for you.

LOOKING GOOD, FEELING GREAT

I never understood how women with babies went out looking as though they had hardly brushed their hair, let alone put together something resembling a coordinated outfit. Well, all those mothers who I cast 'can't you even manage mascara?' glances at can now have their own back. Laying my hands on mascara and lip gloss, let alone having the time to put them on, seems like a major achievement most days. If this sounds familiar, then like me, you can probably do with all the help you can get. The good news is that the nutrients a well-balanced diet provides really can help your hair, nails and skin get back on track after pregnancy.

This said, many women will only really feel good once they have got their weight sorted out. While nobody thinks it is a good idea to launch yourself into a weight-loss plan in the weeks after birth, there will come a time when you know that you are ready to tackle the extra pounds. Not only will you feel good but you will be helping your body get into an optimum place for conceiving again.

LOSING WEIGHT BUT STAYING HEALTHY

It is perfectly reasonable to want to shift 'baby' weight. It is worth remembering that the celebrities who appear in their size 10 jeans only days after giving birth have probably put on very little during their pregnancies and are often in their 20s when 'things' do tend to spring back into place much more quickly. For us mere mortals, it usually takes a bit longer. This is absolutely fine and to be expected since it is recommended that you do not try to shed lots of weight when breastfeeding (or to go on mad diets even if bottle feeding).

When you do feel it is the right time to get back to your pre-pregnancy size it is incredibly important that you do so on a sensible plan. It is hard enough to get all the right nutrients into a normal diet but when you cut calories it becomes a lot harder. Research from Harvard University Scientists in America revealed this in a startling manner recently when they looked at the nutritional intakes of some 300 women participating in a weight loss study. What they found was that, along with their average reduction of 500 calories per day, they also reduced their intake of 12 out of 17 vital vitamins and minerals, putting some at risk of deficiency. When the scientists scrutinised the results more closely they discovered that women follow-ing The Zone Diet, specifically, not only saw no dips in nutrients (compared with slimmers on high-protein or very low-fat plans) but actually found raised levels of nutrients like vitamins E and C (needed, among many things, for helping to keep our skin in good condition) and K, which is essential for strong bones.

The Zone diet is not dissimilar to one based on low glycaemic index principles (supported by many nutrition academics). It also has much in common with the excellent *Total WellBeing Diet* by Dr Manny Noakes.

A typical day from any of these could look something like this:

Breakfast: two boiled eggs with one slice of granary toast and a glass of juice.

Lunch: a large 150g portion of chicken/fish/lean roast beef/hummus/mixed beans with lots of salad vegetables, a few boiled new potatoes and a little olive oil based dressing; plus a piece of fruit.

Dinner: a fairly big portion of grilled salmon (or other protein-based food like turkey, chicken, lean red meat, Quorn or tofu) with lots of vegetables and a portion of noodles (about 80g pre-cooked weight), brown rice or pasta.

Between-meal snacks: a handful of nuts mid-morning and a yoghurt and pear mid-afternoon.

In other words, it is a diet that includes normal foods with slightly larger than usual servings of protein, plenty of vegetables, while keeping an eye on servings of carbo-hydrates. Of course, you will also be cutting out all the usual calorie-packed goodies like crisps and biscuits, chocolate, cakes and fast food.

As I mentioned earlier, I would also include a daily vitamin and mineral supplement to be sure that your between-pregnancies body is in the best shape possible for doing the whole thing all over again!

Chapter Eight

Recipes

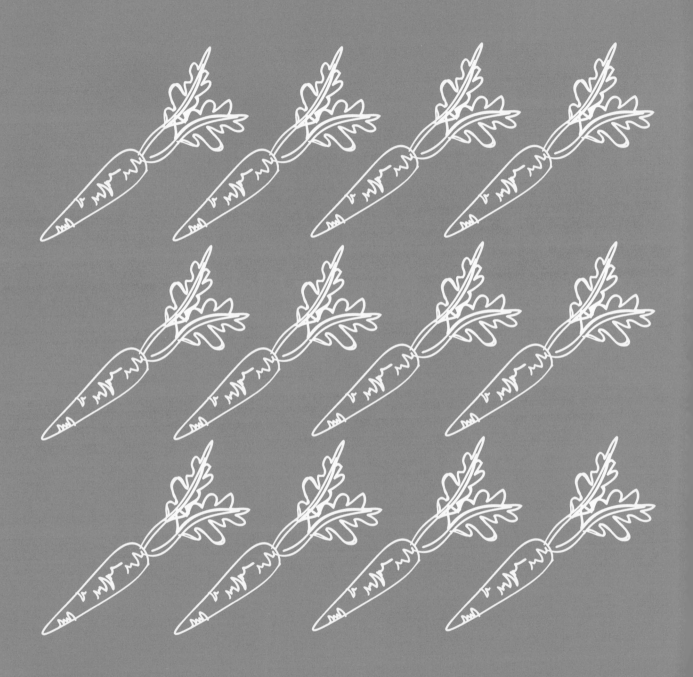

THE WEANING BEGINS! ✶

OK, let's get started. You will tend to know when your baby is ready to move from a milk-only diet to beginning the fascinating journey of weaning. This sees them moving from very soft and loose purées to trying all kinds of new tastes and textures as they gradually progress to 'real' family meals.

Remarkably, the whole process of weaning usually only takes six to eight months. Although it can sometimes feel never-ending, do bear in mind that whatever the setbacks – however much food is refused, spat out and thrown over the side of the highchair – it is a relatively short process. It is also a really precious period of time when you can begin to see your baby's personality emerge, their likes and dislikes and unique funny little ways. I loved the weaning period although there were plenty of times when I thought that I would go a bit loopy if I had to wipe yet more puréed vegetable off the floor and hose down the highchair once again.

So, when exactly do you start? The current advice is to try to wait until your baby is six months of age. Coco was fine waiting until she was at the six-month stage but Freddie was really eager to get stuck in at five months. I waited as long as I could but it began to feel unkind not to get him started. He began his first foray into purées two weeks short of the six-month mark.

Here are some basic tips to bear in mind before you get started:

- Remember that weaning is not a race. Some babies take longer than others. Start slowly and progress at your baby's pace. Don't worry what other babies of the same age are doing. It's only yours that counts!

- Your baby will still be getting virtually all of its nutrients from baby milk, during the first months of weaning, whether it is your breast milk or an appropriate baby formula. Weaning is a process: initially the aim is to get your baby used to taking new flavours and textures, and 'solids', from a spoon. To do this they need to learn to move food from the front to the back of their mouths and then swallow it, rather than using the glugging motion they are used to when knocking back their milk.

- It is not the aim to provide a three course, nutritionally balanced meal from the get-go.

- A good time to try your baby's first purées is after they have had a bit of their milk feed. This way they are not so hungry and will probably have more patience. The lunchtime feed often works best.

- It is best if you are both relaxed so choose the mealtime when this is most likely to be the case. Trying to spoon purées into a baby for the first time when you are rushed, tired or stressed is not a great idea. Babies pick up on these emotions, just like adults, and it will blunt their appetite and make the whole idea of trying anything new stressful and offputting.

- Babies often push their first purées out of their mouth almost as soon as they have taken them from the spoon. They simply don't know what to do with them to begin with and need a bit of practice. Try again gently but if they get upset, stop and try again at the next meal.

- A couple of teaspoons is all you can expect a baby to cope with when you start to introduce purées. Even then, do it only once a day.

- Once babies get into the groove, realising they can move the purée to the back of their mouths and swallow it, you can try purées at two meals and then build up to three in the same day.

- Be guided by your baby. If they seem to want a bit more then, within reason, let them have it.

- If your baby is happy and growing well and seemingly not that interested in starting purées, maybe leave it a week or so before you try again. It is a good idea to have got the ball rolling by six and a half months.

First purées can include:

Vegetables
Fruits
Cereals
Yoghurt and fromage frais (as long as full fat and sugar free)

FOOD HYGIENE AND SAFETY

Whichever foods you introduce it is important to be really fussy about food hygiene. Babies are much more likely to get a dodgy tummy than adults – whose resistance to general bugs around the kitchen is that much greater. As well as the obvious things like hand washing, having clean surfaces, utensils and equipment before making their food, it is also important to clean your baby's hands before starting, not to reuse any leftovers and to clean their highchair thoroughly after each feed.

If you do prepare food in larger quantities for the freezer or for later use, always cool it down within two hours of cooking and then either refrigerate or freeze it in suitable pots. If you do go down the freezing route, make sure you don't leave the food lingering there for months on end. If you haven't used it within three months there are two things to consider: first, you shouldn't use it from a food safety point of view; and second, your baby will probably have moved way past the stage of needing that particular dish. When you do use a home-frozen dish, only ever reheat it once.

When you start weaning, switch your baby from using a bottle to an age-appropriate feeding cup, one with handles and a flexible spout. Make sure that all the parts of the cup are thoroughly cleaned after every use.

10 TOP WEANING TIPS

1. Don't let your concentration waver when feeding your baby. They need to be watched at all times to avoid choking and general distress.

2. Always check for small bones, gristle, lumps of fat and other things that can increase the likelihood of choking.

3. Never serve food hot. It will burn their mouths. Blatantly obvious but worth remembering. This is one reason it is not recommended that you microwave food for babies and toddlers because the temperature can vary through the food and be warm in the one spot that you test but too hot in another.

4. Never try to force your baby to eat. When they open their mouths they are ready. When they have had enough they will stop opening their mouths. If you try to force things they will sense stress and work out that feeding situations are something they can manipulate to illicit a reaction from you.

5. Remember that the weaning process can be messy, especially as they quite rapidly want to join in and put their fingers and hands in the food. It is a good idea to accept this, letting them explore and get involved. They will soon want to wave a little spoon around. Most of the food won't make it into their mouth but try not to stress – it is part of the learning process.

6. Try your absolute hardest to eat with your baby. It can be tricky trying to feed them while ensuring they are safe and actually eating something – but do what you can. Babies need role models from the start.

7. While most of us have to use commercial baby foods from time to time, do your best to make purées, their first meals and family meals at home. They look different, smell different and taste different – almost always for the better.

8. If you are feeling stressed before you sit down with your baby, do whatever it takes to calm down a bit. Put on some calming music, take some deep breaths and consciously try to create a nice atmosphere. Restaurants take a lot of time and effort to make dining experiences nice because it encourages people to relax, eat well and come back another time. It is the same for a baby. If they eat in a relaxed and fun environment they will look forward to the next time.

9. Think variety. As your weaning journey progresses, keep in mind that the more variety you offer now, the more likely your little one is to grow into a child who likes and accepts different flavours and textures.

10. Once your baby is happy taking its first purées, under a close and watchful eye, you can start to offer them foods that they can hold and gnaw on. 'Sticks' of peeled pear, nectarine, peach and banana are good to start with. Cooked and cooled vegetables like carrot sticks, mini corns and green beans (not stringy) are also good. Toast is often suggested but it is worth being aware that bread can add quite a bit of salt to your baby's diet. If they get a real liking for it this can be quite significant.

The British Dietetic Association have a useful guide regarding what kind of foods to offer when weaning and when to introduce them.

First-stage weaning foods (at six months) should be puréed. Good examples include fruits, vegetables, potatoes, yam, meat, cheese and custard. No foods containing gluten, such as bread, should be given.

Second-stage weaning foods (six to nine months) should be a thicker consistency with some lumps and given with some soft finger foods. Good examples to add to those above include fish and well-cooked eggs, bread and cereals. The American Dietetic Association suggests appropriate consistency lean red meat as well.

Third-stage weaning foods (nine to twelve months) now include the same foods in a mashed, chopped or minced consistency. It is also good to add firmer finger foods.

Fourth-stage weaning foods (from twelve months) include mashed and chopped family foods and, again, more finger foods.

Vegetable and fruit purées

These make great first-stage weaning foods. As your baby moves through the stages you can begin to serve them as thicker consistencies and eventually, as the fruit or vegetable itself. It is amazing how often mums go to loads of effort to provide a wide variety of purées and then drop half of those fruits and vegetables when it comes to serving them 'whole'.

These purées introduce an array of wonderful colours and flavours to your baby's diet. They may recognise some of these flavours from their time in the womb or through your breast milk if you had a diet rich in these vegetables at the time.

FIRST PURÉES

The first- and second-stage purées below can be altered in their consistency by adding cooking water, breast milk or formula to thin them or by adding appropriate baby cereals to thicken. You will need to blend less as weaning progresses to ensure the mixture gets a little lumpier. There are lots of ideas for you to try. Babies move pretty swiftly through the soft purée stage to slightly lumpier versions and you are soon able to include finger foods.

Beneath each purée recipe I've noted why it is particularly good from a nutritional point of view. Obviously your baby is only having small quantities but, hopefully, as they grow they will continue accepting the foods to which they have become accustomed. Once they are able to consume more of them, the nutrients they provide will take on a bigger significance.

FIRST-STAGE PURÉES

Cereals to mix with purées

There are a variety of starchy carbohydrate cereals and grains that you can use when weaning your baby. Added to vegetable and fruit purées, they make a change in texture and taste. They also have the advantage of making a watery food slightly thicker as well as making a meal more filling. I used to give my children a starchy, carbohydrate-based breakfast once they were up to having 'food' at each meal: usually a baby porridge mixed with some puréed blueberries, apricots or apple with some banana mashed.

Baby rice

There is nothing very inspiring about either the taste or texture of baby rice but it has the advantage of being one of those foods least likely to cause an allergic reaction. Make up according to pack instructions.

Good because:

✓ It is naturally gluten free.

✓ It is bland so can be mixed with vegetable and fruit purées without affecting their taste too much.

Oatmeal

Oatmeal that has been very finely milled is another nice option for babies. Follow the cooking instructions on the pack and serve, testing the temperature first.

Great because:

✓ Oatmeal has the advantage of being slightly more tasty than baby rice or home-cooked white rice.

✓ It also boasts more vitamins and minerals and some soluble fibre.

Cooked rice

Again, it is naturally gluten free. You can start your baby off with white rice, which you boil and then cool down and blitz in a hand blender with a little breastmilk or formula until you get the right consistency.

Cornmeal

Cornmeal or maize, as it is also known, is often found in baby cereal. It can be used to make a simple first cereal base to which you can add vegetable or fruit purées. Follow pack instructions to make it up.

Great because:

✓ *Cornmeal has the advantage of being easy to digest and is naturally gluten free.*

Millet

Millet is a nutritious small yellow grain with a mild yet slightly sweet flavour. Used as a first weaning food in many African countries, it can be cooked using one serving of millet to three of water.

Good because:

✓ *Millet has small amounts of iron and selenium, minerals needed for energy and immunity.*

✓ *It also provides some folic acid needed for good nerve health.*

FIRST VEGETABLE RECIPES *

ROOT VEGETABLES

Basic purée method

Once you know how to make a basic carrot purée, you can adapt the same method for all of the other vegetables below. I have put some special tips in with each. On the advice of a very experienced children's nanny I know, I always sieved my children's first purées (using a plastic sieve to avoid metal ones getting tainted) to ensure that they were completely smooth. As weaning progresses, and your children get used to thicker and lumpier textures, you can stop sieving.

Carrot purée
. . . .

Carrots are an excellent first-stage weaning food, sweet and usually well received.

**1–2 medium-sized carrots (young ones are sweeter), peeled and sliced
water to boil**

Peel or scrape the carrot until skin is removed and slice. Pop into a small pan of boiling water: just enough to cover the carrots. Put on the lid and simmer for 15–20 minutes until tender. Remove and drain the cooking water into a small bowl or cup. Purée the carrots with a tablespoon of the cooking water (or a little breast milk or baby formula) until the purée is smooth and soft. To check for consistency: it should drop easily off the spoon if you turn it upside down. Add a little more cooking water or baby milk if you need to. Put a few spoonfuls in a bowl to serve and the rest can be frozen in two or three sections of an ice-cube tray. When you want to use these, defrost and add a little cooled boiled water if you need to alter the consistency.

Great because:

✓ *Carrots cause very few reactions in babies or adults. It is therefore a particularly safe vegetable with which to start weaning.*

✓ *Carrots contain the orange pigment, beta carotene, which is converted into vitamin A in our bodies. This vitamin helps with development of the eyes and the mucus membranes in our nose and throat, which, in turn, helps our immune system to fight infections like colds.*

Sweet potato purée

Sweet potatoes taste deliciously sweet and are generally very well accepted by babies as a first weaning food.

1 medium-sized orange-fleshed sweet potato, peeled and chopped
water to boil

Peel the sweet potato and chop into small chunks. Pop into boiling water and cook for 15 minutes until soft (pierce with a sharp knife to test). Drain and follow the carrot purée method.

Great because:

✓ *Sweet potato is one of the few vegetables that gives us vitamin C, vitamin E and beta carotene. All are important antioxidant super-nutrients, which can help build your baby's immune system and general health.*

Potato purée

This purée is a great base that can be mixed with other vegetables, especially green ones like broccoli, which can be a bit loose on their own.

1 large potato, peeled and chopped
water to boil

Peel and cut the potato into small chunks. Cook for 15–20 minutes until soft, using the minimum amount of water. Then follow the carrot purée method.

Great because:

✓ *Potatoes give us vitamin C needed for development of a strong immune system.*

✓ *Useful for second-stage purées to help with consistency.*

Parsnip purée

Try to find a young parsnip as the old ones can be a bit tough.

1 medium-sized parsnip, peeled and chopped
water to boil

Peel and chop the parsnip into small chunks. Place a pan of boiling water and cook for about 15 minutes. Once soft, drain and follow the carrot purée method.

Great because:

✓ *Parsnips can taste nice and sweet, making a good first weaning food. Like potatoes, they make a good base, as weaning progresses, to which you can add other vegetables.*

Butternut squash purée

I find butternut squash to be quite a challenge to peel but it is worth having a go because the results are really tasty.

1 small butternut squash (about 300g), peeled and chopped
water to boil

Cut the squash into quarters, then cut them across again. Once you have manageable-sized chunks in your hand, you can then get to grips with them and peel the skin off with a sharp knife. Next, remove the seeds and throw them away and chop the squash pieces into small chunks. Place in a small pan of boiling water, put on a lid to partly cover it and then simmer for about 20 minutes until soft. Then follow the carrot purée method.

Great because:

✓ *Butternut squash is usually sweet tasting and gives us carotenes for healthy lungs and immunity.*

Pumpkin purée

Pumpkin is a good one to try in purées when it is in season. It's tough to peel but is naturally sweet and tasty.

1 small pumpkin, peeled and chopped
water to boil

Follow the method for butternut squash purée above.

Great because:

✓ *As with squash, pumpkins give us a variety of health-boosting carotenes including the yellow pigment lutein, which appears to help to protect eyes from sun damage.*

Yam purée

Yams also make great purées.

1 yam, peeled and chopped
water to boil

For method follow the sweet potato purée recipe.

Great because:

✓ *Yams give us some vitamin C needed for immunity, as well as a little iron for energy.*

✓ *Although soft and easy to eat, yams do provide some fibre and are rich in potassium needed for good blood pressure control.*

Note on swede purée: I didn't give this to my babies because it is one of those vegetables that can trigger wind in some people. The last thing you want is your baby suffering with this when they are just starting weaning. There are plenty more gentle vegetables to use at the start. You can include swede in their diets as they get older (for example, mashed in with potatoes) and see if it affects their digestive systems then.

Broccoli purée

. . . .

Broccoli is one of those 'superfoods', which we know we should eat. But do bear in mind that research has shown that some people have taste buds sensitive to bitter foods. Cooking it for a minimum time helps to reduce this trait. It is also worth noting that the bitter-tasting super-nutrients in broccoli are also present, in smaller amounts, in other vegetables of the same family such as cauliflower, watercress and sprouts.

80–100g broccoli florets from a small head of broccoli
water to boil

Pull the florets apart (cutting them loses more of the vitamin C) but do cut off any tough-looking stalky bits. Put in a small pan of boiling water (with just enough to cover half the florettes) and place a lid on it. Cook for about 10–12 minutes until the florettes are soft. Drain and follow the carrot purée method.

Great because:

✓ *Sulforaphane, a super-nutrient in broccoli, appears to increase levels of enzymes that detox pollutants and carry them out of harm's way in the urine.*

✓ *Broccoli also gives us indoles, which seem to have a role in blocking cancer. Obviously the last thing you think about with babies is cancer but with weaning we are trying to introduce foods that they will eat and benefit from throughout life.*

✓ *Broccoli also has protective carotenes, vitamin C and some energy-boosting iron.*

Cauliflower purée

Cauliflower, although in the same family of vegetables as broccoli, is not as bitter-tasting so is often more acceptable to babies.

80–100g cauliflower heads
water to boil

Pull the florets off the cauliflower, cutting off the big tough stalks. Follow the carrot purée method, making a purée with a little of the cooking water, breastmilk or formula.

Great because:

✓ *Although cauliflower has fewer super-nutrients than broccoli, it also is believed to have cancer-fighting properties.*

Courgette purée

A mild-tasting vegetable making it an ideal first purée.

1 large or 2 smallish courgettes, trimmed and sliced
water to boil

Trim both ends of the courgette and slice. Boil in a small pan of water, drain well and blend. You won't need to add any cooking water or milk because courgettes are quite watery themselves.

Great because:

✓ *Courgettes have a low allergenicity, which makes them a good first purée.*

FIRST FRUIT PURÉES *

Pear purée
· · · · · · · · · ·

Soft varieties of pear are best for weaning babies. Some people give their baby very soft raw pear, blended. My preference is to wait until your baby is ready for first finger foods before giving it to them raw.

2 medium-sized soft, sweet pears, peeled, cored and sliced
2 tbsp water

Peel the pears, remove the core and slice. Place in a small pan with a well-fitting lid along with about 2 tbsp water. Simmer gently for about 5 minutes. Either mash very well with a fork or blitz with a hand blender until really smooth, adding a little extra water if you need to make the purée a bit looser.

Great because:

✓ *Pears are unlikely to trigger allergic reactions and are one of the most safe first weaning foods.*

✓ *Pears are also good for soluble fibre.*

Mashed banana

Banana is a fabulous first weaning food because it comes in its own sterile packaging. Ripe and sweet tasting, it is brilliantly transportable.

1 ripe banana
a little breastmilk or baby formula

Peel banana and mash it (or blitz with a hand blender) with a little baby milk to get a lovely, soft, easy-to-eat texture.

Great because:

✓ *Bananas have what experts call 'low allergenicity'. In other words, they very rarely lead to an allergic reaction.*

✓ *Bananas also give us lots of potassium for well-controlled blood pressure.*

Apple purée

Apples come in so many varieties that you can rotate the types to help a baby get used to new flavours, gradually introducing slightly less sweet varieties as time goes by.

2 sweet eating apples, peeled, cored and sliced
1 tbsp water

Peel, core and slice the apple, placing it in a small pan with a well-fitting lid. Add about 1 tbsp cold water, cover and simmer gently for about 6–7 minutes by which time the apple should be soft. Mash well with a fork or blitz with a hand blender until really smooth. Add a little extra water if you need to make it slightly looser.

Great because:

✓ *Apples supply a host of super-nutrients including quercetin, a potentially viral-busting nutrient, as well as soluble fibre. Both are useful as babies grow into toddlers, older children and adults.*

✓ *Growing up with the idea that 'an apple a day keeps the doctor away' is no bad thing!*

Mango purée

Mangoes, when ripe, are naturally sweet and beautifully textured. They are usually a favourite with babies, who like the sweet taste and silky feel of the fruit in their mouths.

1 very ripe mango, peeled and sliced
1 tsp water (optional)

Peel a ripe mango and slice the juicy flesh into a bowl, discarding the stone. Blitz with a hand blender adding either any excess mango juice or a little water.

Note: this fruit can be a little tricky to prepare. One of the best ways is: hold the mango and slice the juicy flesh away from the large stone so that you are left with two pieces, both still with their skin intact. Do this over a bowl to catch the juices. To get the mango away from the skin make 'hedgehogs': cut the mango lengthways into about four slices. Take care to cut through the flesh but not the skin. Next do the same crossways, making a hatched pattern. Now invert the skin, pushing the cubes of mango upwards. These are then easily cut away and plopped into a bowl.

Great because:

✓ *A mango's beautiful orange pigments have beneficial antioxidant properties.*

✓ *While babies only get a small amount of these super-nutrients when first weaning, you will be paving the way for them to enjoy these bright, colourful, health-boosting foods in the future.*

Avocado purée
· · · · · · · · · · · · ·

Avocados are literally bursting with goodness. A perfect first food but remember:
they don't keep well in the fridge and you cannot freeze them.

1 small ripe avocado, peeled, mashed and de-stoned
1 tbsp breastmilk or baby formula

Peel the avocado and remove the stone. Scoop out the ripe, soft flesh and mash along with the baby milk. It can be a little gloopy as a first purée and so many need a bit more milk than you think to get the right consistency. Blend only what you need (eat the rest yourself, sliced in salad or sandwich or on its own as a nutritious snack).

Great because:

✓ *Avocados give us a range of B vitamins for developing nerves.*

✓ *They are full of healthy, unsaturated fats, which do not raise cholesterol in the blood. It is never too soon to be thinking about the kind of fats you give your little ones. Children fed a junky diet have been found to have cholesterol build-ups on their arteries from as young as three years of age.*

✓ *Infants can progress to having avocado as a finger food, as long as it's not too ripe; then when they are older instead of butter in sandwiches or on toast.*

Peach purée

It has been shown that bright colours literally help to lift your mood. I see no reason why this also shouldn't be the case for babies and toddlers, so giving them vibrant foods like peaches has to be a good thing!

2 ripe peaches, peeled, de-stoned and chopped
water to blanch
1 tbsp excess juice, breastmilk or baby formula

Cut the peaches in half over a bowl to catch the juice, then cut again into quarters (having removed the stone) and peel with a very sharp knife. (You can use the peel to put into a smoothie for yourself.) This is tricky as the peaches tend to be squishy and you end up losing a lot of the juice. Alternatively, you might find it easier to put the peaches into a pan of briskly boiling water for about 60 seconds (in the same way you might skin tomatoes). Once you have taken them out, run under cold water so that you can handle them. The skin should now come away quite easily. Chop the fruit and blitz with a hand blender, adding some of the saved juice and/or a little baby milk if you need to. You can cook the peach slices for a few minutes before puréeing if you want to but they are safe to eat uncooked. (Make sure you have washed your hands, the peaches and knife before preparing the purée.)

Great because:

✓ *The colourful orange pigments in peaches have antioxidant properties that are useful from the earliest age.*

Apricot purée

It is lovely to use fresh, sweet apricots when in season.

**3 juicy fresh apricots, peeled, de-stoned and chopped
water to blanch**

Blanch your apricots first, if peeling proves too fiddly, and go for the biggest apricots you can to cut down the hassle. Once your apricots have been peeled and de-stoned, blitz them fresh with a hand blender or cook for a few minutes in a little water until you have a smooth consistency.

Great because:

✓ *Apricots have quite a mild flavour and are usually well-accepted by babies.*

✓ *Like other orange-coloured fruits and vegetables they also give us a range of carotenoid antioxidants. The eyes of babies and children are particularly vulnerable to damage by ultraviolet radiation from the sun (even on cloudy days) and so getting them used to these foods is good from the earliest age.*

Nectarine purée

Another popular fruit with babies, when in season.

2 ripe nectarines, peeled, de-stoned and chopped
water to blanch

Prepare as with peaches, either skinning fresh or blanching first before peeling over a bowl to catch the juices. Blitz with a little of the juices or boiled water with a hand blender to get a smooth and loose consistency. Serve.

Great because:

✓ *Along with peaches, apricots, nectarines and papaya, nectarines contain the wonderful antioxidant carotenoids which may help protect tiny eyes as well as developing lungs.*

Papaya purée

If you can get hold of a ripe papaya from your local fruiterers or supermarket then this could not be a simpler first weaning food.

1 ripe papaya, peeled, seeded and chopped
1 tbsp breastmilk or baby formula

Cut in half lengthways, scrape out the seeds and peel. Blitz the fruit with a little baby milk with a hand blender until you get the right consistency.

Great because:

✓ *Papaya is really great for vitamin C, which all bodies need for a strong immune system and for producing good quality skin. By six months a baby's vitamin C stores are running out and they need topping up from their diet.*

✓ *Papaya gives us brightly coloured antioxidant pigments which may help protect the body from sun damage from the inside out.*

Plum purée

You really do need ripe plums because if they are tart they will probably be rejected swiftly by your baby. You can use plums canned in natural juice if you would like to, although as these have been cooked at a high temperature during the canning process they will have lost some of their flavour. Still, they are a good standby and useful when plums are not in season.

3 ripe plums, peeled, de-stoned and chopped
water to blanch
1 tbsp cooled boiled water

Blanch the plums in boiling water and remove the skin. Cut in half, remove the stone and then blitz with a hand blender, adding water for the correct texture.

Great because:

✓ *Plums give us wonderful purple pigments, which is thought to help to protect blood vessels and heart health.*

STAGE-TWO PURÉES *

Once you and your baby are up and running on the purée front, which normally takes a couple of weeks, you can begin to get a bit more adventurous. By introducing single purées initially, you will have a good idea which ones suit your little one and will have weeded out any that may have caused a slight reaction after several occasions of trying them out.

Now you can try some of these ideas, which introduce a few new vegetables and fruits, combining those they have already enjoyed. Remember that frozen vegetables and fruits can be really useful too. Good quality brands freeze their produce within a very short time of harvesting, which means that they retain much of their vitamin C and many of the B vitamins too.

SECOND VEGETABLE PURÉES

Watercress and carrot

Make sure that you wash the watercress really well before using and cut off the tough, stalky bits. Like broccoli, watercress contains bitter-tasting super-nutrients. Although the sweetness of the carrots can help to tone them down, they can still be too much for some babies. If they really don't like it, wait for a few days and try again. If rejection continues, wait again and try again. If they are a super-taster (see p.34) it may be that they will never learn to love it.

2 carrots, peeled and sliced
small handful of watercress
water to boil

Wash, peel and slice the carrots and cook for 10 minutes in a small amount of water until soft. Add the watercress and cook for a further 5 minutes. Drain, retain some of the water and purée with a hand blender . Add a little of the water if you need to thin it down.

Great because:

✓ *Watercress has been shown to have potential cancer-fighting properties and is great for lutein which may help protect eyesight.*

✓ *It also gives us iron needed for energy and vitamin C to help its absorption.*

Pea, mint and courgette purée

A real immune-booster with the mint adding an extra layer of flavour.

100g frozen peas
1 courgette, sliced
a few leaves of mint
water to boil

Cook the peas in a very small amount of water with mint and after 5 minutes, add the courgette and cook for a further 5 minutes. Drain, retaining the cooking water and remove the mint leaves. Purée with a hand blender, adding some of the water if you need to thin down the consistency before serving.

Great because:

✓ *Peas are good for vitamin C, a nutrient needed for building strong immunity.*

✓ *They also introduce some iron and fibre in a gentle way.*

Broccoli and pea purée

Even if your baby has given broccoli the thumbs down before, they might well like this as the peas bring sweetness to the dish.

100g broccoli florets
100g fresh or frozen peas
water to boil

Break the broccoli into small florettes and cook in a small amount of water for 8–10 minutes until soft. Add the peas and cook for a further 5 minutes. Drain, keeping back some of the cooking water. Purée with a hand blender adding a little of the water if you need to.

Great because:

✓ *Broccoli and peas are packed full with super-nutrients and vitamins.*

Pumpkin and tomato purée

Tomatoes are a wonderful base for so many dishes. It is good to introduce them early on so that when your baby gets to the stage of eating with the family they are used to the taste.

100g pumpkin, peeled, seeded and chopped
1 medium or 2 small tomatoes, skinned, seeded and chopped
water to boil
1 tbsp olive oil

Make the pumpkin purée as per method in the first-stage purée section (p.116). When you get to the point where it is cooked through, drain. Next, blanch the tomatoes for about a minute and then remove skins and chop. Next, heat 1 tbsp olive oil in a small pan and add the chopped tomatoes. Cook for 5 minutes, stirring most of the time. Once soft, add to the pumpkin and purée, adding a little breastmilk or formula to get the right consistency.

Great because:

✓ *Tomatoes are full of lycopene, a red pigment that seems to have protective roles in our bodies. For boys, good intakes throughout life may lower the risk of prostate cancer.*

✓ *Lycopene is also good for heart health and may help protect skin, from the inside out, from sun damage.*

Courgette and green bean purée

A mild-tasting purée that is a favourite with babies.

1 large courgette, trimmed and sliced
a handful of frozen green beans
water to boil

Trim the courgette and cut into slices. Cook in a small quantity of water in a pan with a fitted lid for 5 minutes until soft. Cook the beans separately following pack instructions. Drain both vegetables and blend.

Great because:

✓ *This dish provides your baby with vitamin C for strong immunity.*

Celeriac and parsnip purée

Celeriac is a root vegetable that tastes a little bit like celery but with nutty overtones. Mixing it with parsnip tones it down a bit and I found that both of my children were happy to give it a go. It is worth a try because celeriac is a lovely vegetable and you can make sure that you save some for yourself too.

Half a small celeriac, peeled and chopped
1 parsnip, peeled and chopped
water to boil
1 tbsp breastmilk or formula (optional)

Top and tail both the celeriac and parsnip, then peel and chop into similar-sized pieces. Celeriac skin is tough and you have to discard quite a bit to remove it completely. Cook both vegetables in boiling water for about 20 minutes until soft, then drain and blitz with a hand blender. Add a little of the cooking water or baby milk to get the right consistency.

Great because:

✓ *Celeriac provides you with potassium, needed for good blood-pressure control.*

✓ *Parsnips give us some immune-boosting vitamin C and useful amounts of folate, the B vitamin needed for healthy nerves.*

Beetroot and potato purée

· ·

Beetroot is a fantastic colour bringing a whole new look to your baby's food repertoire

1 small beetroot, washed
1 small potato, peeled and chopped
water to boil
1 tbsp breastmilk or formula (optional)

Wrap the whole beetroot in foil without topping or tailing or piercing the skin. Bake for about 40 minutes until you can pierce it easily with a knife. Prepare and cook the potato as per the first-stage purée method (see p.115). Combine the cooked beetroot and potato and blitz with a hand blender until you get a smooth purée, adding some baby milk or cooking water if you need a thinner consistency.

Great because:

✓ *Beetroot contains interesting super-nutrients, which research suggests may be helpful in heart health.*

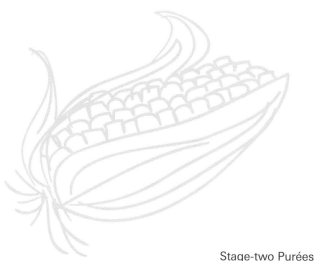

Parsnip and carrot purée

These vegetables both have a mild but sweet taste with the different flavours combining well.

1 medium-sized parsnip, peeled and sliced
2 medium-sized carrots, peeled and sliced
water to boil
1 tbsp breastmilk or formula (optional)

Peel and slice both root vegetables, making the pieces approximately the same size. Cook in boiling water for 15–20 minutes until soft, then drain and blitz with a hand blender. Add a little of the cooking water or baby milk to get the right consistency.

Great because:

✓ *Carrots help to give your baby beta carotene, which can be converted into vitamin A. This is needed for the development of the eyes and the lining of the mucus membranes, which helps to prevent invading cough and cold viruses from entering the body.*

Sweet potato and broccoli purée

The sweetness of the sweet potato can help to tone down the bitter notes of the broccoli super-nutrients.

1 medium-sized sweet potato
100g broccoli florets
water to boil

Prepare both vegetables separately as per methods in the stage-one purées and then combine and blitz with a hand blender before serving.

Great because:

✓ *This is a super superfood purée if ever there were one. Brimming with eye-protecting carotenes, it is also full of vitamin C for a strong immune system and betacarotene which is converted into vitamin A needed for healthy eyes.*

Cauliflower, parsnip and carrot purée

The soft and sweet nature of the parsnips and carrot helps to tone down the stronger flavour of cauliflower and can transform this vegetable from being unacceptable to well liked.

1 portion of each of the cauliflower/parsnip/carrot individual purées

For method see first-stage weaning section (p.119, 115, 113). Next, blend the purées together for a tasty three-in-one version.

Great because:

✓ *Cauliflower, like broccoli, has super-nutrients that help the body make important detoxing enzymes.*

✓ *This purée also gives us carotenes (from the carrots) for eye and immune system health.*

To give added flavour and to stretch your baby's palette further ...

Once used to these types of combinations you can try adding the following herbs and spices to those purées that contain the following ingredients:

mint to pea

thyme to parsnip

parsley to carrot

basil to tomato

nutmeg to spinach

chives to sweetcorn

You may also like to try adding:

apple to parsnips

orange juice to carrots

spring onion to potato

All give an extra flavour dimension to the purées.

SECOND FRUIT PURÉES

Blueberry and apple purée

This is a good time to introduce blueberries to your little one. They really are nature's superfood.

2 handfuls of blueberries
1 sweet apple
water to boil

Make the apple purée found in the first-stage purées section (page 121). When almost ready, add the blueberries so they get a couple of minutes of simmering to soften up. Blitz with a hand blender and serve. You can also try adding a little banana for a slightly more substantial version.

Great because:

✓ *Blueberries carry on surprising researchers with their plethora of potential health benefits,*
  which include protecting brain health and helping to dampen down inflammation in the body.

Apple and pear purée

A very gentle low-allergy combination of fruits.

1 portion of each of the apple and pear purées

Follow the method for the apple and pear purées (see pages 121 and 120). You can cook both fruits together to save time or simply mix single ones that you may have in the freezer.

Great because:

✓ *These fruits give your baby some useful soluble fibre, which helps to keep blood-sugar levels steady.*

Strawberry and peach purée

When the strawberries are ripe this is a really delicious combination. It has a slightly different texture provided by the presence of the tiny strawberry seeds.

4 fresh or frozen strawberries, hulled
1 portion peach purée

Wash and hull the fresh strawberries (or defrost frozen ones) and then blitz with a hand blender without cooking. Add them to the peach purée in the first-stage purées section (page 124).

Great because:

✓ *This purée's vibrant colour is appetising and it gives your baby vitamin C as well as super-nutrients such as ellagic acid, a powerful antioxidant.*

Peach, pear and mango purée

This combination is delicious and vibrantly coloured to capture a little one's interest.

1 small peach, peeled, de-stoned and chopped
1 small pear, peeled, cored and chopped
½ ripe mango, peeled, de-stoned and chopped

Now your baby has got past first-stage single purées you can simply blitz with a hand blender the very ripe, uncooked fruits, making sure you peel, stone or core them first. You can use half a peach, half a pear and quarter of a mango for the purée, giving the rest to older children as finger foods or polishing off yourself as a quick, nutrient-boosting snack.

Great because:

✓ *Mango and peach provide carotenes which are believed to be useful for eye and skin health.*

✓ *These carotenes are also helpful in promoting a healthy immune system. Converted into vitamin A, they help to build strong mucus membranes, which help to block viral infections from entering the body and setting up infections.*

Apricot and peach purée

A delicious, gentle combination for one of your baby's first forays into multi-flavoured purées.

1 portion apricot purée
1 portion peach purée

Combine both of these stage-one purées (see page 125 and 124). Serve.

Great because:

✓ *This combination is good for potassium, needed to maintain good blood-pressure control.*

✓ *Both fruits provide antioxidant pigments believed to promote good general health.*

Melon and raspberry purée

Raspberries are really tasty when ripe and, with the many little lobes that make up each fruit, are surprisingly good for fibre.

1 slice sweet, ripe honeydew melon, peeled, seeded and chopped
1 handful of ripe raspberries

Wash the melon thoroughly before slicing and carefully rinse the raspberries. Chop and seed the melon, add the raspberries, then blitz with a hand blender to make the appropriate texture of purée.

Great because:

✓ *Raspberries have double the fibre of strawberries because each raspberry is a small cluster of up to 125 fibre-rich seeds, each housed within a juicy lobe.*

✓ *They are good for ellagic acid, an antioxidant also found in strawberries, thought to help fight cancer.*

✓ *They provide immune-boosting vitamin C and the B-vitamin folate, needed for healthy nerves.*

Avocado and banana purée

Avocado is such a perfect first food and, when the flesh from half a small fruit is combined with banana, it makes a delicious fruit combo.

½ ripe avocado
½ ripe banana

Mash the fruits together or blend for a smoother consistency. Remember that avocado needs to be used immediately as it doesn't keep well in the fridge and you cannot freeze it.

Great because:

✓ *Avocados give us B vitamins for developing nerves, monounsaturated fats, and plant stanols: substances that help to lower cholesterol – a useful function as they grow older.*

✓ *They also give us vitamin E for healthy skin while bananas are good for blood pressure-controlling potassium.*

Apple, pear and banana purée

Tasty and creamy-textured, this can be offered when your baby is ready to move on to a purée of slightly firmer consistency.

1 portion apple purée
1 portion pear purée
½ ripe banana

Mash the banana and mix with the apple and pear purées (for method, see pages 121 and 120).

Great because:

✓ *The apples and pears provide soluble fibre while the bananas offer a type of fibre that can be used as food by good bacteria in the gut. This is definitely an all-round 'good gut' purée.*

Blueberry and banana purée

By seven months, my son was happy to accept blueberries when prepared this way.

1 handful blueberries
½ banana
1 large tbsp Greek yoghurt

Add the blueberries to the banana and Greek yoghurt and blitz with a hand blender. (It is best to use Greek yoghurt because normal yoghurt is often runnier in consistency.) If you want to make the purée slightly easier to digest you can pop the blueberries in a very small amount of water to simmer for just a minute or two to soften the skins a little.

Great because:

✓ *Blueberries are bursting with super-nutrients, including the potentially cancer-fighting chlorogenic acid, and anthocyanin pigments that give blueberries their beautiful blue colour.*

✓ *These antioxidants, along with others such as vitamin C, are believed to have brain-protecting properties.*

Pear and prune purée

Prunes are quite strong tasting so the pear helps to tone this down a little.

1 dried prune, stoned and soaked in water for an hour
1 portion pear purée
water to boil

Simmer the prune in a little water for 7–10 minutes. Add to the pear purée and blitz very well so that the skin is completely broken down. Serve.

Great because:

✓ *Prunes contain sorbitol, a sugar-alcohol (don't worry: they do not contain any actual alcohol). This helps to gently encourage the passage of stools through the colon.*

Once your little ones are used to these flavours, you can try adding:

Vanilla to peaches, pears and apricots
Cinnamon to apple
Mixed spice to plums, apricots, mango and peaches
Zest of lemon and orange to banana and blueberries
Mint to raspberry and melon

Note: It can be fun growing your own herbs with your toddlers. It is lovely watching them sprout and grow in front of your eyes. Herbs can be grown outside but also in window boxes. Fresh herbs have a lovely taste and although dried herbs can definitely be useful to add flavour to dishes, they can be up to two years old by the time you open the pack and use them.

MEAT, FISH AND PULSES *

Once your baby has mastered some first purées (don't worry, you do not have to wade your way through all the recipes before you move on to this next stage), it is time to add a bit more texture and some new ingredients, which can include:

Puréed cooked chicken, turkey, beef and pork or white fish like cod and coley

When using meat or fish, check and check again to make sure they contain no bones! I always sieve the purée to be really sure.

Great because:

✓ *These foods add protein and useful minerals such as iron from red meat and dark poultry meat. For this reason, dietitians in America recommend introducing these as first weaning foods.*

✓ *These protein foods are also more filling and sustaining than fruits and vegetables alone.*

Cooked pulses like chickpeas and lentils

Pulses can be added if well cooked and well puréed. If used as a first weaning food make sure they are well sieved.

Great because:

✓ *Pulses are useful as a provider of minerals, like iron, which help to replace an infant's stores, which by six months of age have been used up. Iron is needed for energy, brain development and concentration.*

Obviously, all of the above foods are cooked without salt.

Usually, within a month or two of starting purées, a baby can move on to chewing lumps and soft finger foods they can feed themselves. It is normal for them to begin mastering these skills between six and nine months, and from six months to be drinking from a beaker rather than a bottle.

NINE TO TWELVE MONTHS

By this stage in their weaning process, babies will be used to chewing minced or chopped food as well as the harder textures of finger foods. By twelve months they are even able to begin to enjoy chopped or minced family meals (theirs being cooked minus salt and sugar of course). At this point, you need to think through their meals to ensure that they contain the same elements that are provided in grown-up meals.

Try and provide the following combination (with the appropriate texture for your infant's stage of weaning):

protein: from, for example, milk and dairy produce, meat, fish, eggs, pulses or tofu

carbohydrates: from, for example, pasta, potato, rice, noodles, yam, low sugar/salt breakfast cereals like porridge or bread (but be aware of its salt content)

vegetables and fruits: a wide variety of colour and with the most appropriate textures.

At this stage you should be aiming to get your child into a good routine of three (sometimes four) meals a day. A main course and a small pudding is appropriate. The latter can be a good source of fruit, and milk puddings (or dishes with custard) are good for bone-building calcium even though they add a little sugar to their diet.

Between meals, a healthy, age-appropriate snack will be needed. Check out my snack chapter for ideas. Be prepared to alter quantities of snacks to ensure they are not so filling that your little one is no longer hungry at mealtimes. This can seem like fussy eating when, in fact, a child is simply not hungry.

As solid food begins to play a larger role in their day, an infant will need a bit less milk. I gave my children two formula feeds a day up until the age of one, and after this, continued with two toddler milk feeds: one after breakfast and one before bed.

Once your little one is getting confident with lumpier textures you can progress to the Main Meals section (page 177).

BREAKFASTS *

It is the mantra we all know so well that I hardly feel the need to repeat it (but, for the sake of dotting 'i's and crossing 't's, I'd better do so): breakfast is the most important meal of the day! Of course, the real truth is that it is only 'one' of the most important meals of the day but, the point is, breakfast is often not taken as seriously as other meals and this is a great mistake.

Here are some reasons why breakfast is important:

1. Research shows that children who skip breakfast or who eat very little at the start of the day are at a disadvantage compared to those who have something 'proper' to eat before leaving home. The sooner you start the habit of getting your child to sit down and expect some good quality food and drink at the start of the day, the easier the process will be. And of course, children are learning from the earliest age, not just once they get to school. A good breakfast will no doubt help everything from learning to walk and talk to developing coordination and feeling stable and steady in their moods.

2. If these claims for the benefits of breakfast seem a bit tall, then it is worth understanding why they have been made. If you haven't eaten anything since the previous night, by the time morning comes, the levels of blood sugar reaching the brain are below optimal. This doesn't mean that you or your children are going to keel over immediately after getting up but that during the morning, certain parts of their memory may not be working as well as they might. During the night the body manages to supply enough sugar to the brain by calling on supplies to keep it going. By the time the morning

comes, energy needs shoot up to supply your muscles, which are needed to get you out of bed and moving around. This can mean that on rising, there is a relative shortage of sugar getting to the brain. And blood-sugar levels regulate a variety of brain functions, including learning and memory.

3.   Scientists have shown that children who eat breakfast score better in tests that involve matching up familiar figures. Eating breakfast has also been shown to have beneficial effects on reaction times and problem solving as well as improved scores in maths tasks.

4.   As well as academic tests, children have been found to score better in creativity tests and tests of physical endurance during the morning if they have had a good and nutritious breakfast, rather than the opposite.

5.   Not surprisingly, research has shown children feel more hungry after a small (rather than a substantial) breakfast leading them to say that they felt 'bad' during the morning.

All this evidence, showing the benefits of giving your children a good start to the day with a nutritious breakfast, has led the scientist Dr David Wyon to summarise things as follows:

'I think that parents who don't make sure that their children have eaten a good breakfast are, in effect, handicapping them in their school work in several different ways. Our studies show that children's school performance is affected by their nutritional status in the short term. Therefore, it is important that children are fed breakfast in some way.'[2]

OK, so your tots may not yet be in school, but laying down good habits now will stand them in good stead for when they are. Here are ten breakfast recipe suggestions you may like to try. Of course, we all have our staple breakfast favourites and if you find that you are already in a good groove with nutritious things your little ones enjoy, you may not want to rock the boat. However, you can always adapt the recipes to suit a child's particular tastes and try a few if you like the idea of them.

Apricot and chocolate muffins

Muffins are a great way to introduce new fruits to your child's diet. Once they have enjoyed apricots in a muffin, you can serve the 'real thing', saying it's what they have for breakfast. Or you can put some fresh versions of the fruit on the same plate. Other fruits to try in muffins include blueberries and raspberries. A word of warning: the muffins don't taste massively sweet so may seem a bit underwhelming to the adult palate. We tend to have them with a glass of milk-based, homemade fruit smoothie, spreading them with ricotta cheese to make them more substantial.

250g plain wholemeal flour
2 tsp baking powder
30g granulated fruit sugar
1 egg
30ml vegetable oil
150ml whole milk
180g ripe apricots, de-stoned and chopped
20g milk chocolate, cut into chips

Put muffin cases into a muffin tray (this makes about 8–10 small muffins). Heat the oven to 180°C/gas 4. Put the flour and baking powder in a bowl and mix well. Next add the sugar and mix again. Make a 'well' in the middle of the mixture. Crack the egg into another bowl and add the oil and milk. Whisk well, then pour into the 'well' in the mixture in the other bowl. Stir it briskly and, once well mixed, stir in the apricot and the chocolate chips. Spoon equal amounts into the muffin cases and bake. Check after 25 minutes. If ready, a sharp knife will go in and out with no mixture attached. If you need another 5 minutes, return to the oven until done. Cool and serve. Makes 10 mini- or 4 regular-sized muffins.

Great because:

✓ *The chocolate is only present in a tiny amount but is enough to make the muffins feel a bit special while the apricots provide a little fruit. If you have them with a milk-based smoothie and ricotta it means that you boost the protein content of the meal to make it more filling.*

Super-quick porridge with mango

A wonderfully sustaining meal. Offer your children some toast as well to make sure that they have had enough to eat.

> **40g porridge oats**
> **140ml milk, semi-skimmed or whole, depending on age**
> **40g dried mango, cut into small pieces**

Mix all the ingredients together and make the porridge in the traditional way in a pan on the hob. (You can always make porridge the night before and heat it up in the morning to save time.) Once cool enough to eat, add a little more milk and serve. Makes two small or one bigger child-sized portion.

Great because:

✓ *Porridge is wonderfully filling as oats provide slow-release energy and the milk gives you a protein boost.*

Peanut butter toast with crunchy apple

Try to buy peanut butter that has no added sugar and the minimum amount of salt. Obviously this is not suitable for any child with a peanut allergy. Little ones tend to get on best with smooth versions but it can stick to the roof of their mouth so make sure that they eat it with the apple and have a drink with it too to keep their mouth moist.

1–2 slices wholemeal toast
2 tsp peanut butter
1 small crunchy apple

Toast the bread and spread with peanut butter. Cut into finger-food sized pieces. Cut the apple into slices and serve with peanut butter toasted strips.

Great because:

✓ Peanuts give us protein, which is filling, as well as lots of important nutrients like vitamin E and iron for concentration and energy.

Grilled bananas with fromage frais

This is a quick-to-prepare breakfast but you do need something else with it to make it a substantial enough way to start the day. A toasted slice of malt loaf is a good accompaniment.

1 tsp vanilla essence
1 tbsp orange juice
1 medium-sized banana
1 tbsp fromage frais or Greek yoghurt

Cut a piece of foil big enough to wrap a banana. Sprinkle foil with the vanilla essence and half of the orange juice. Peel a large, medium-ripe banana and place on the foil. Brush with the rest of the orange juice. Grill for 5 minutes. Serve with a blob of Greek yoghurt or fromage frais. One banana serves two small children or one older child.

Great because:

✓ *It is a good way to have fruit at breakfast and is warming in winter. Bananas are good for potassium, an important mineral for healthy blood pressure throughout life.*

Oatcakes and avocado

This very fast and simple breakfast is deceptively nutritious and filling.

½ small ripe avocado
2 oatcakes
1 handful grapes, sliced

Scoop the flesh from the avocado, mash it, then spread on top of the oatcakes. You will probably need to break the oatcakes up into finger-food sized pieces. Slice the grapes into a size your children can manage (don't give to very young ones, who may choke) and serve in a ramekin or small bowl so that they can eat the grapes alongside the avocado oatcakes.

Great because:

✓ *Oatcakes provide slow-release energy while avocados are both filling and have a surprising contribution to make to fibre as well as vitamin intakes, such as folate for healthy nerves and vitamin E.*

Oatibix and apple

Oatibix is one of the best ready to eat breakfast cereals around for children, containing some of the lowest levels of added salt and sugar yet still tasty enough to tempt them. We usually follow this with some mashed banana and yoghurt to makes sure that the children have had enough to eat.

**1 Oatibix
½ sweet apple, grated or puréed
milk, semi-skimmed or whole (depending on age)**

Put the Oatibix in a small bowl. Place the grated or puréed apple around the Oatibix and pour on the milk. Let it soak in a bit and then serve.

Great because:

✓ *Having an oat-based breakfast means that you are not having wheat at every meal. Otherwise, there is a small risk of developing an intolerance due to wheat overload.*

Scrambled eggs with tomatoes

For the tomato:

**1 very ripe tomato, chopped
1 tbsp olive oil**

For the egg:

**1 egg
1 tbsp milk
1 tbsp olive oil
1 slice of wholemeal toast**

Place the tomato in a small pan with the oil and cover with a well-fitting lid. Cook over a low heat for 10 minutes until the tomato has browned a little and is nice and mushy. For the scrambled eggs: place all the wet ingredients in a small, non-stick pan and stir with a wooden spoon over a medium heat. Toast the bread. Once the eggs are well cooked (this is necessary to avoid the unlikely, but possible, problem with salmonella food poisoning), serve on top of the toast and with the mushy tomatoes. Serves 1.

Great because:

✓ *Eggs are wonderfully nutritious, being packed with protein and providing a small amount of vitamin D for strong bones, which is found in few other foods. The tomato means that you are serving a portion towards your child's 'five a day'.*

Fruity Toast

This is a quick weekend breakfast if you are dashing out to make the most of a nice day. To make it substantial enough, try serving with a milk-based smoothie.

> **2 slices fruit loaf**
> **50g ricotta cheese**
> **1 fresh, ripe peach, de-stoned and sliced**

Toast the two slices of fruit loaf and spread with the ricotta cheese. Serve with the slices of peach on the side of the plate. Serves 1.

Great because:

✓ *Fruit loaf makes a change from toast and goes well with ricotta. It is something slightly sweet for breakfast without actually being loaded with sugar. It is digested slowly so that it gives a gentle supply of energy in the morning ahead.*

Pancakes with strawberries

Another weekend breakfast, this time for when you have a bit more time to spare. Try serving with a milk-based smoothie.

For the pancakes:

125g self-raising flour (wholemeal if you can)
1 tsp caster sugar
1 egg
185ml milk
Oil to brush frying pan

For the strawberries:

100g strawberries, hulled and cut into quarters
100g strawberry-flavoured fromage frais

Sieve the flour into a bowl and stir in the sugar. Make a 'well' in the middle and drop in the egg with half of the milk. Begin mixing. When thick and creamy and all the flour has been beaten in, lightly stir in the rest of the milk. Heat a small non-stick frying pan and brush with oil. Pour over enough of the pancake mixture to thinly cover the base of the pan. Cook until the pancake is golden underneath, then flip over and cook again until the second side puffs up. Mix the strawberries with the fromage frais and place a spoonful on the pancake. Roll up and serve. Serves 4.

Great because:

✓ *You are serving fruit in an interesting way and the wholemeal flour means that your pancakes are a bit more filling than they would be with white. A milk-based drink alongside your pancakes will mean that you boost protein intakes along with bone-building calcium.*

Eggy bread

This is a way of serving eggs that, to put it simply, doesn't look like eggs!

2 slices wholemeal bread
1 egg
1 tsp brown sugar (optional)
1 pinch cinnamon (optional)
1 tsp olive oil
1 blob Greek yoghurt
favourite berry purée

Leave two slices of wholemeal bread out overnight. Whisk the egg with the sugar and cinnamon. Dip the slices of bread into the egg mixture and fry in a non-stick frying pan brushed with a little oil. Cook for 2–3 minutes each side, then remove from the pan and cut into strips. Mix the Greek yoghurt with your child's favourite fruit purée, then let them dip the eggy bread into the fruity yoghurt.

Great because:

✓ *This is a filling and nutritious breakfast that also introduces fruit on the side as a purée. Older children may prefer to have fresh fruit alongside. Slices of peach work really well with this breakfast and provide fibre and protective carotene pigments. Although the recipe uses a teaspoon of sugar, which is 4g in weight, this is almost a third less than the sugar in a bowl of chocolate rice cereal.*

Carrot cake

This may seem like an unusual way to start the day but it is fun for a change and quite filling. Try serving it with Greek yoghurt for even more sustenance.

150g plain wholemeal flour
1 tsp bicarbonate of soda
1 tsp baking powder
120g granulated fruit sugar
250g carrots, peeled and grated
2 eggs
150ml olive oil
1 tsp vanilla essence

Grease and line an 18cm cake tin. Put the oven on at 180°C/350°F/ gas 4. Sieve the flour, bicarbonate of soda and baking powder into a bowl and stir in the sugar. Peel and grate the carrots and stir into the mixture. Lightly beat the eggs and add along with the olive oil and vanilla essence. Beat until everything is well combined, then pour into the cake tin. Check after 30 minutes and, if risen and firm to the touch, it is ready. It may need another 5 minutes or so until it gets to this point. Once cooked, remove from the oven and, after a few minutes of resting, turn out and allow to cool. Try serving the cake with a blob of plain Greek yoghurt.

Great because:

✓ *How else can you get your children to eat carrots for breakfast? The granulated fruit sugar combined with the wholemeal flour and carrots means that this will not give a big sugar rush even though it is a 'cake'. The eggs and oil help to make it filling and if you serve it with Greek yoghurt, this will make a surprisingly sustaining start to the day.*

Fruit smoothie

· · · · · · · · · · · · ·

A brilliant accompaniment to any breakfast. Use any of your child's favourite fruits (banana, mango, berries, apricots, peaches – you choose!). These can be fresh or canned in natural juices or frozen and defrosted. In summer months you can try adding a pinch of freshly ground cardamom for an uplifting boost and in winter a pinch of mixed spice gives a warming twist. Infants under one should not be given honey as it can cause serious food poisoning.

> **150g fruit of your choice**
> **75g natural yoghurt**
> **200ml milk (whole for the under 2s, semi-skimmed for the 2–4s or full-fat fortified soya)**
> **1 tsp clear runny honey**

Put all of the ingredients into a bowl and blitz with a hand blender until you have a smooth, velvety consistency. Pour into a large glass and drink! Serves 2 small children or one older child/adult.

Great because:

✓ *A homemade smoothie can give your child several servings of fruit for the day and, because they are freshly made, they contain all the nutrients, unlike shop-bought ones, which, whatever the brand and however fresh they purport to be, can be up to 20 days old before you buy and use them.*

SNACKS AND QUICK LUNCHES *

SNACKS

Healthy snacks are an important part of young children's daily food intake. This is because their stomachs are relatively small, which makes it is hard for them to stock up with enough food at mealtimes to see them through the three or four hour stretch until the next. Regular snacks mean that your children have an energy lift between meals and they are an opportunity to introduce extra nutrients and yet more flavours, textures and variety to their diets. They also can play an invaluable role in coping and dealing with phases of fussy eating (see page 29).

Making sure that snacks are nutritious as well as tasty and appealing can be tricky, but hopefully these ideas will help you along. Some are quite filling while others are lighter. You will be able to judge when and what is most appropriate on the day.

The former are useful if your little one hasn't eaten particularly well at a certain meal of if they are being especially active, whereas a lighter snack may be good on a hot day when they are also having a juice and perhaps an ice lolly as a treat as well, or when they have had an especially filling meal beforehand.

Chocolate and apricots

No one advocates giving children loads of chocolate, but working on the basis that if you ban things, children seem to want them even more, I give my children a little bit of chocolate now and then. Hopefully they won't grow up thinking it has magical properties or feel bad about eating it. This little snack provides a bit of balance with the flavours mingling nicely.

2 dried apricots, chopped
6 chocolate buttons, cut into quarters

Chop the apricots into small pieces and as far as you can, chop the buttons into quarters as well. Put into a little bowl and mix them up (or into a small plastic tub and shake) before serving. Obviously, this is only suitable for children once they are completely safe eating small pieces of food like raisins and there is no risk of them choking.

Great because:

✓ *Apricots provide iron for energy.*

✓ *The protein and milk in the chocolate may help to reduce the stickiness of the apricots from causing tooth decay.*

✓ *Chocolate has been proven to be less likely to cause tooth decay than toffees and chewy sugary sweets.*

Oatcakes with cream cheese and cucumber sticks

. . . .

You can take this snack out and about by making the oatcakes into a cream cheese 'sandwich' and wrapping the cucumber sticks in foil to make everything transportable.

1 oatcake
25g cream cheese
1 small cucumber

Spread the cream cheese onto the oatcake. Slice the cucumber into sticks. Serve all together in a little bowl or on a small plate.

Great because:

✓ *Many oatcakes are low GI, which means they raise blood sugar slowly after eating and keep energy levels on an even keel.*

✓ *Having them with cream cheese and cucumber means that you can stick with one oatcake (half an oatcake sandwich). This is important for young children because a single one can easily contain 0.2g of salt and snacking on large numbers can contribute quite a bit of salt to their day's intake.*

✓ *The cucumber counts as one of their 'five a day'.*

Celery sticks filled with peanut butter

You can make these in minutes at home or prepare them and take with you when going out. Peanut butter can tend to get stuck to the roof of small children's mouths. For that reason, it is a better snack for slightly older children. The celery does add some moisture to help prevent this happening though.

1 large celery stick
1 tbsp peanut butter (with no added sugar)

Trim the celery stick and then fill the centre of it with the peanut butter. Slice into finger-food sized portions and serve.

Great because:

✓ *Peanut butter gives your children protein, which they need for growing as well as some iron for energy.*

✓ *The celery counts as one of their five fruit and vegetables for the day.*

Satsuma and cheddar

1 satsuma, peeled, segmented and sliced
20g mild cheddar, chopped

Peel the satsuma and break into segments, cutting them in half as you go and removing any pips. Cut the cheddar into small pieces and serve with the satsuma in the same bowl or on a small plate.

Great because:

✓ *The proteins and calcium in the cheddar are good for bone health, but they also help to buffer the acid of the satsuma, which may otherwise erode tooth enamel.*

Melon slices with raspberries

1 slice melon (any type)
1 handful raspberries (or 50g if canned)

Almost any melon works well with raspberries. You can purée the raspberries (canned ones in fruit juice work well for this) and pour over chunks of melon served in a bowl. Alternatively, simply slice the melon into finger-food sized pieces and put them in the same bowl as a handful of raspberries and let your little ones pick on the fruit.

Great because:

✓ *Raspberries are packed with easy-to-eat fibre and lots of super-nutrients plus immune-boosting vitamin C.*

✓ *This snack counts towards your children's 'five a day' of fruit and vegetables. If they have a big serving, it could count as two portions.*

Avocado with breadsticks

A good morning or afternoon snack, it can be an easy-to-digest nibble before bed as well.

½ small avocado, flesh mashed
2 breadsticks
1 tsp fromage frais (optional)

Simply scoop the flesh from a small avocado and mash in a bowl to make a 'dip'. You can add a little plain fromage frais to make it go further if you wish. Serve with the breadsticks, letting the children scoop up the dip with them. Strips of toasted pitta bread or vegetable sticks can also be used.

Great because:

✓ *Avocados are full of nutrients, from B and E vitamins to monounsaturated fats.*

Ricotta cheese with apple and pitta strips

Ricotta has a lovely mild taste and makes an ideal home-based snack food.

1 mini pitta bread
1 small apple, sliced finely
50g ricotta cheese

Toast the pitta slightly until warm but not too crispy and cut into strips. Next, wash and slice the apple into quite fine slices. Spread the ricotta cheese onto the pitta strips and serve on a small plate or in a bowl with the apple slices.

Great because:

✓ *Ricotta cheese is low in salt but good for protein and calcium, both of which are essential for strong bones.*

✓ *Apples give us immune-boosting super-nutrients and fibre. Their presence means you can use just one mini pitta thereby keeping salt levels under control.*

Fruit scones with ricotta

Here is another use for ricotta cheese that goes down well with little ones.

½ fruit scone
1 tbsp ricotta cheese
2 strawberries, sliced

Toast half the scone (it may just squeeze into the toaster but, alternatively, can go under the grill) and then spread with the ricotta. Serve with strawberries on the side.

Great because:

✓ *This is a 'treat' and yet does not have the fat or added sugar of a traditional cream tea.*

✓ *The strawberries provide super-nutrients and fibre plus immune-boosting vitamin C.*

Fruit loaf with cream cheese and grapes

1 slice fruit bread
1 tsp cream cheese
1 small handful grapes

Spread the fruit loaf with the cream cheese and cut the grapes in half. You can try laying the grapes on top of the fruit loaf or simply serve them separately by the side.

Great because:

✓ *Fruit loaf is quite sweet-tasting but not loaded with lots of added sugar (most comes from the dried fruits).*

✓ *It has about 0.3g salt per slice. Having it with cream cheese makes it a filling snack so you can stick with one slice.*

Grapes with melon

Another really simple but popular fruit combination that makes a light snack. If you need to make this snack more substantial, add some small pieces of cheddar too.

6 black grapes, quartered or halved
1 slice melon, chopped

Cut the grapes into quarters or halves depending on their size and cut the melon into small chunks. Mix together and serve with a small fork.

Great because:

✓ *Grapes are bursting with antioxidants. Black grapes have more than green so I try to serve them.*

✓ *Melon is rich in water and can help with hydration on hot days.*

Cheese and pineapple

An old-fashioned, yet ever-tasty combination, these nibbles are loved by children as much as by adults.

1 x 20g chunk mild cheddar (or your children's favourite cheese)
4 chunks pineapple (fresh or canned in fruit juice)

Cocktail sticks are not a good idea to let children loose with! I give cheese and pineapple to my children on a plate (one plate each to avoid rows) with their toddler forks. This way they can spear the sections of cheese and pineapple themselves. They may not actually eat both together, but the flavours still mix well in the mouth.

Great because:

✓ *Cheese is always good for bone-building calcium and its proteins and milk content help to buffer the acidity of the pineapple, which may help tooth health.*

Toasted wholemeal pitta and peanut butter

A more substantial snack, it is most suited to older children who can cope better with the texture of peanut butter. The cherry tomatoes provide some moisture, which makes it less likely to stick to the roofs of little mouths. Obviously it is not suitable for children with peanut or general nut allergies.

½ wholemeal pitta bread
2 tsp peanut butter
2–3 cherry tomatoes

Toast the pitta bread until warm but not crisp. Cut lengthways and spread the peanut butter inside on one side. Close up and serve as a 'sandwich' along with some cherry tomatoes to pick on.

Great because:

✓ *The pitta gives some good slow-release energy.*

✓ *Peanut butter provides iron, protein and calcium for energy and bone health.*

Dried apricots and sultanas

A highly portable light snack, which you can pack up and take with you on an outing. Add a mini Babybel cheese to make it more substantial. Do try and buy dried fruits that have not been preserved with sulphur dioxide.

2 dried apricots, chopped
Sultanas

Cut the dried apricots into the same size pieces as the sultanas and put into a plastic bag or small pot. Give them a good shake to mix before serving.

Great because:

✓ *The apricots are good for slow-release energy and for iron, which itself is an energy-boosting nutrient.*

✓ *Sultanas add extra sweetness. Together with the apricots they count as one serving of the 'five a day' fruit and vegetables for the day.*

Fresh apricots and strawberries

Another tasty fruit mix for your little ones to pick on. You could try substituting dried apricots for fresh as well.

2 fresh apricots, de-stoned and chopped
4–5 strawberries

Cut the apricots in half, removing the stone, and then cut into quarters. Remove the hull from the strawberries and cut into the same size pieces as the apricots. Mix in a bowl and serve with a teaspoon or baby fork.

Great because:

✓ *Fresh and dried apricots give us useful amounts of fibre and dried give us iron.*

✓ *Strawberries are bursting with vitamin C, which helps the iron be absorbed.*

Frozen berry yoghurt

You need to plan ahead to make this nutritious and tasty snack. Making a larger quantity means that you can have some ready in your freezer for next time.

1 handful frozen berries
1 individual-sized yoghurt
1 tsp granulated fruit sugar

Blitz the berries while still frozen and mix in the fruit sugar. Stir into the yoghurt and pour into a lolly mould. Freeze for a few hours and then serve.

Great because:

✓ *Yoghurts give us calcium for strong bones and healthy muscles.*

✓ *Berries are wonderful for immune-boosting vitamin C and a host of health-giving super-nutrients as well as gentle forms of fibre.*

Apple juice lollies

I find that my children enjoy lollies even in the winter, something I find rather odd. Of course, they are even more of a hit in summer. You can use any juice to make them.

150ml cloudy apple juice

Simply pour the juice into a lolly mould and freeze!

Great because:

✓ *Cloudy apple juice has more super-nutrient flavonoids compared with the clear. These flavonoids are useful for heart health.*

✓ *One lolly counts as one of the 'five a day' portions we need.*

Apple and blackberry lollies

During the blackberry season we make up a batch of stewed apple and blackberry. Simply blending canned apricots or pineapple with some of the natural juice they are preserved in also works well.

1 handful blackberries
1 sweet eating apple, sliced
granulated fruit sugar to taste

Slice the apple (and peel) and cook gently in a little water with the blackberries for about 10 minutes until soft. After it has cooled, add some granulated fruit sugar to taste and then pour into a lolly mould and freeze.

Great because:

✓ *Blackberries are one of the few fruits that are good for vitamin E, a nutrient needed for development and heart and skin health.*

Fromage frais and berry layers

This is a nice snack to have ready in the fridge because it doubles up as a tasty, standby pudding as well.

100g plain fromage frais
1 handful chopped berries (fresh, frozen and defrosted, or canned)
3 tsp granulated fruit sugar

Put a layer of fromage frais on the bottom of 2 ramekins. Divide the berries into 2 portions and spread on top of the fromage frais. Sprinkle 1 tsp granulated fruit sugar over each one. Top with the rest of the fromage frais and finish by sprinkling the top of each with a little extra granulated fruit sugar or a little brown sugar. Put in the fridge for at least 1 hour before serving. This gives the fruit, fruit sugar and fromage frais time to mingle.

Great because:

✓ *This snack provides a portion of fruit towards your child's 'five a day'.*

✓ *Fromage frais provides calcium for strong bones.*

QUICK LUNCHES

In addition to the very quick risotto (page 221) and ciabatta pizza (page 198) in the Main Meals section, here are seven more quick lunch ideas for you to whip up. Of course, they can easily be used for suppertime as well. Most are suitable from toddler stage up, varying quantities as necessary.

Baked potato

There is almost nothing as simple as serving a baked potato with a tasty and nutritious filling. For little ones at the first weaning stage, I like the method from page 216 where you bake the potato, then scrape out the cooked insides, adding a little olive oil and passing it through a ricer to make it smooth and very easy to eat. As children get a bit older, a nice way to have baked potato is to scoop out the insides and mash with lemon juice. It sounds odd, but it makes the potato soft and fluffy. You can then mix it with various fillings and put it back in the skin or simply serve on a plate without it. Baked potatoes only take five minutes to prepare but around 75 minutes to bake in the oven. Estima and Marfona potatoes are the best for baking. I microwave my potatoes for a quick lunch but do oven bake if you have the time (see below).

Conventional method:

Heat your oven to 200°C/390°F/gas 6. Wash the potato skins clean, prick them all over with a fork, lightly brush with oil, then put on a baking tray. After an hour, prick the potato to see if it is cooked all the way through. If not, leave for a bit longer. If you want to speed up the cooking you can push a skewer through the potato, leaving it there while it bakes. They should then only take 45 minutes.

Microwave version:

In a microwave a potato takes about 6 minutes on full power in an 800w oven, turning after 3 minutes. Before cutting the potato open let it sit for a couple of minutes.

Good fillings:

Ricotta cheese with chives

Tuna and sweetcorn with chopped parsley

Avocado and tomato

Salmon and cream cheese

Hummus and chopped cucumber

Pitta bread and wraps

Suitable for: over-twos

The great thing about the fillings on page 173 is that they can all also be used to fill pitta breads and tortilla wraps, adding a little shredded lettuce if you like.

Gnocci

Gnocci can be blended down for second-stage weaning and can be chopped up as your little one gets more confident and able to handle pieces of food. You can buy ready-made gnocci in the chill cabinet of supermarkets. It is fantastically easy to cook, taking under five minutes in boiling water. You can add a variety of sauces to make a quick and tasty meal:

- homemade tomato sauce (page 183) and parmesan

- homemade tomato sauce and ricotta cheese

- half-fat crème fraiche and cooked spinach

Cheese on toast with sliced tomatoes

Toast a slice of bread and on it lay slices of tomato. Top with some grated cheddar and pop under the grill for 5 minutes or until the cheese is melted and slightly browned on top. Serve with some iceberg lettuce drizzled with Balsamic vinegar.

Avocado with pitta, cucumber and cherry tomatoes

Peel an avocado and cut the flesh into slices. Place on a plate with pieces of sliced cucumber and some cherry tomatoes cut in half, along with some strips of toasted pitta. Serve and let children eat with their fingers.

Noodles with peas and sweetcorn

Cook some plain noodles in a pan of boiling water, following instructions on the packet, and quickly cook a handful each of frozen peas and sweetcorn and drain. A few minutes before removing from the heat, add the peas and sweetcorn. When cooked, drain and place in a bowl. Pour a little olive oil, and sprinkle Parmesan cheese over the noodles. Mix well and serve.

Rice and vegetables with chickpeas and salmon

Take a pack of Uncle Ben's quick-cook rice. Once cooked, stir in 1tbsp canned chickpeas and a little flaked, cooked salmon per child, along with 1tbsp cooked mixed frozen vegetables.

MAIN MEALS *

Most children like fish fingers, peas and chips if this is what they are used to. There is nothing wrong with this once a week or so. But most of the time, surely we should be giving children the kind of food we would love to sit down and tuck into ourselves? The idea that children should be eating pizzas cut into shapes like a train or made to look like a face seems a bit contrived to me. OK for a party maybe, but why on earth should we be giving children the message that 'their' food is different from 'grown-up' food?

The sooner we start to make and give our children real food, the kind we are happy to eat, the better. If we eat good food together at the same table, children are less likely to develop food fads or get stuck in a rut: expecting nothing but processed-looking and processed-tasting food. This way they are less likely to over-eat on calories and under-eat on wholesome carbohydrates, good quality protein, vegetables and fruit. And they'll get lots of minerals, vitamins and super-nutrients to help really good health, from the earliest days of weaning until they themselves are grown-ups making their own food decisions.

In this book, you will not find meals that pander to children who 'don't like vegetables' by deliberately hiding them. If they happen to be chopped up and not an obvious part of a dish, that's fine, but that is a world away from messing around with bits of broccoli in an attempt to pretend it isn't broccoli. (If your children genuinely don't like this vegetable after many times of trying, there may be a good reason for this, which you can read about in my fussy eaters chapter on page 29.)

What you will find are tasty, healthy meals passed down through generations of Franco's (my children's daddy) and my own families. Some are straightforward, old-fashioned dishes from my typically mixed-up British background (with a bit of English, Scottish and Irish thrown in). Others are everyday Italian meals: some originating from the Abruzzo region of Italy, where all the very best pasta is made; others from Naples, the home of the classic Neapolitan sauce used in so many pasta dishes. Then we added our favourite dishes from other countries to the mix.

My children, Coco and Freddie, are used to sitting down to anything from a colourful roast dinner (Freddie, who's one, has his carefully chopped up, of course!) to a bowl of pasta with a simple but wonderfully flavoursome tomato sauce. I'm not saying they always eat it. Of course they don't. They are children. Some is spat out; some still lands on the floor; and some doesn't get tasted if they are having an off day. But, on the whole, they usually have a go. Moreover, they are realising that mealtimes are a social occasion where they sit down with as many people as possible (this may just be you, some older children, a grandparent or friend), enjoying the occasion as well as the food.

This is all that can be expected of any busy mum and I hope that these recipes are a help in allowing you to do the same as often as you can.

I do sometimes use very small amounts of salt in my children's food if I think it is really going to make a difference to whether they will actually eat it or not. This is not as controversial as it first may sound. Why? Because if I do, I use only a tiny amount and then make sure that they do not get salt in other foods that day. I know that bread or pitta, certain breakfast cereals, snacks of cheese or oatcakes quietly notch up salt intakes during a normal day without most people giving them a second thought. I hope that now you've been made aware of it, that you too will be able to balance the salt in your child's daily diet.

The servings information for each recipe relates to an adult-sized portion. It is simpler that way as I have no information as to the age of your children or how big their appetites are. You will be able to scale down the amount to suit them. Many recipes are suitable for blitzing with a blender and so are good for little ones of one year or more. Others are ideal for mashing or chopping. Do remember, though, that a baby's weaning period goes quite quickly and what might not have been suitable a month previously, may quickly become spot on, so keep reviewing which recipes will work for you.

STORE CUPBOARD ESSENTIALS *

There are three essential recipes I couldn't do without: herb salt; stock; and tomato sauce. The staple recipes below can be made in bulk and used, when stored appropriately, over the days and weeks ahead. I then give suggestions on how to use them in a wide range of meals.

Herb Salt
. . . .

One way of using a little salt and adding lots of flavour is with herb salt. This wonderful seasoning of Franco's (which you can make up, then store in an airtight jar) provides lots of flavour to dishes when you use it to season meat, fish and pizzas in place of salt. You only need a tiny amount to make a big difference to taste.

8g dried oregano
6g dried marjoram
4g dried sage
12g dried thyme
12g dried rosemary
8 dried red chillies, seeded and chopped
80g coarse sea salt

Place all ingredients in a blender and blend for 5 seconds at a time for 5 or 6 times.

Great because:

✓ *Gram for gram, herb salt has a third less salt than traditional salt and much more flavour.*

Stock

· · · · · ·

You need to make this when you know that you will be at home for six hours so that you can allow the stock to simmer away so that the flavours really develop. This may seem like a long time but you can, for example, start it off in the afternoon and let it simmer until bedtime. You can also do part of the cooking in a slow cooker, if that is easier for you, transferring the contents from the saucepan to the slow cooker after the first two hours of cooking. (However, don't panic: there is a 'quick stock' version, which follows this recipe if these options are impossible.)

Whichever way you do it, making your own stock is well worth the effort. When it is ready, you will have a delicious and deep-tasting, salt-free stock that can be used to make an array of dishes. It can be used immediately, kept in the fridge for a few days, or simply frozen in small containers until you are ready to use it.

1 whole chicken, fat cut off but skin on
4–5 celery sticks
2–3 large onions, peeled and chopped
3–4 carrots, peeled and chopped
1 small head of garlic, cut in half
2 bay leaves
4 tomatoes, cut in half
water to cover chicken

Put the chicken into a large pan and add all the other ingredients. Cover with cold water and heat at the lowest temperature possible on your hob, without a lid. Let it gently come to the boil, which will take about 2 hours, then let it simmer for 4–5 hours. Check on it every hour or so and skim off any greyish-looking bubble bits. Drain the stock and throw away the vegetables. Take the meat off the chicken. This can be used to make soups, stir fries or added to rice dishes.

Quick stock

. . . .

When you don't have time to make stock the long way, this is a great alternative. It is still tasty and delicious, but only takes 30 minutes of simmering. It can be used to make any number of dishes from soups and stews, casseroles and pasta sauces. One that we all love in our family is the traditional Italian 'pastina', which is really soothing and warming (see below).

4 chicken wings
1 onion, peeled and chopped
2 sticks of celery
2 carrots, peeled and chopped
water to cover chicken

Put all the ingredients in a medium-sized pan and bring to the boil. Simmer with the lid off for 20 minutes. Take the chicken wings out and remove any meat you can from the bones.

Drain into a bowl, discard the vegetables, and the stock is ready to use.

Tomato sauce – the real thing

You need to allow three hours in the oven for this sauce so, as with the stock, plan ahead and think of a good time to make it when you will be at home. I have included a quicker version (which follows this recipe) but the 'real thing' is really, really worth the effort. At the end, you will have a really stunning and delicious sauce, which can be used for a huge array of wonderful dishes.

1.5kg ripe tomatoes (plum are best, the riper the better)
4–5 tbsp olive oil
1 clove garlic
½ tsp salt
1 handful basil leaves

Heat your oven to 125°C/250°F/gas ½. Place the tomatoes on a baking tray that is large enough for the tomatoes to fit snugly but not touching, side by side. Pour over enough olive oil to just coat the bottom of the tray and so that each tomato has been coated while pouring. This seems to be about 4–5 tbsp but use a bit more if you need to. Put in the oven and leave for 3 hours to roast. Once roasted, remove and blend with the garlic, salt, and a handful of fresh basil leaves. The basil leaves and the slow-roasted tomatoes should give the sauce a really delicious creamy, sweet flavour but add some more olive oil or salt if you need to. It is amazing how this can change the taste and bring the sweetness out further. Once happy with the flavour, you can use the sauce right away, keeping some in the fridge or putting into containers to freeze. This sauce gives just a tiny amount of salt per tablespoon.

Great because:

✓ *Tomato sauce is a wonderful way for children to have one of their 'five a day' of vegetables and fruits (a tablespoon's worth being around one portion).*

✓ *It is packed with lycopene, the red antioxidant pigment believed to be helpful in protecting the skin from sun damage. The slow cooking and the oil makes the lycopene especially easy to absorb.*

Quick tomato sauce

*When you don't have time to make tomato sauce 'the long way',
this is a pretty good alternative.*

600g good quality passata
50ml extra-virgin olive oil
1 bunch basil
2 garlic cloves, peeled
100ml water
Pinch salt

Put all the ingredients into a food processor and blitz until a smooth consistency. Put in a smallish pan and bring to the boil. Put lid on askew and simmer for 30 minutes on a low heat. Remove from the heat and stir. Adding 100g of ricotta will sweeten it a little.

In this book you will find 12 quick recipes for dishes that use this tomato sauce. (I do suggest you make 'the real thing' as it tastes much nicer):

SOUPS *

Chicken noodle soup

350ml stock (page 181)
100g skinless chicken breast, finely sliced
30g vermicelli pasta
4 button mushrooms, sliced
1 spring onion, finely chopped
1 clove garlic, peeled and crushed
1 pinch black pepper (optional)
2 tbsp fresh coriander, chopped

Put your homemade stock (or 350ml hot water and half a low-salt stock cube) in
a medium saucepan to simmer. Add the sliced chicken breast and vermicelli pasta
and let the soup gently simmer for 8 minutes. Add the button mushrooms, spring
onion and a clove of crushed garlic (optional) to the soup. Season with black pepper
(optional) and some freshly chopped coriander. Allow all to simmer for 2 more minutes. Serve immediately. Serves 1.

Pastina

· · · · · · · ·

This is a lovely and traditional 'soupy' Italian pasta dish, which my children love. It is warming, comforting and nutritious – and great for little ones when weaning (it can be blended) or 'whole' when a bit older.

40–50g pastina (tiny little 'star' pasta) per child
homemade stock
1 soft tomato, chopped
2 handfuls of peas
1 handful cooked chicken, chopped
1 egg per child, cracked and gently whisked (optional)
1 tsp extra-virgin olive oil
1 tbsp Parmesan cheese, grated

Cook the pastina in the stock (using stock in place of the amount of water suggested on the pack cooking instructions) and add the tomato, peas and chicken. Allow it to simmer until the final version is 'sloppy' but not too liquid (if that is the case, keep simmering until more stock has evaporated). Just before serving add the whisked egg and cook for a few minutes. Then stir in the extra-virgin olive oil and grate in some Parmesan.

Great because:

✓ *Once you have the stock and the pasta, you can add any number of ingredients to make the pastina look and taste different. It is versatile and easy to make.*

Chicken soup

A great way of using up the chicken leftovers, including the carcass, after a family roast.

For the stock:

1 chicken carcass, fat removed, meat shredded

3l water

zest of 1 lime

1 onion, peeled

1 carrot

1 stick of celery

1 tsp red peppercorns

2 sprigs thyme

1 sprig parsley

1 bay leaf

For the soup:

2 tsp extra-virgin olive oil

1 red onion, roughly chopped

stock (see above)

2 garlic cloves, peeled and roughly chopped

1 handful green beans

1 sweet potato, peeled and cubed

1 sweetcorn, kernels cut off the husk

1 pinch salt

2 tbsp white or brown rice, cooked

1 handful basil, torn

1 handful mint

lime wedges, to garnish

To make the stock: place the chicken carcass in a large saucepan and cover with about 3l water. Add the lime zest, onion, carrot, celery, 1 tsp red peppercorns, with the thyme, parsley and bay leaf tied up with a piece of string. Bring to the boil gently, then cover and simmer for about 3–4 hours, removing any scum. Strain and let cool. Refrigerate overnight, then remove any of the fat on top.

To make the soup: pour a little olive oil into a large saucepan and heat, then add the onion and cook for 15 minutes on a very low heat until soft. Add the stock and the garlic and bring to simmering point. Add the green beans, sweet potato and corn, and season with a little salt.

Simmer for about 8–10 minutes. Add the rice and cook for a further couple of minutes.

Decorate with the basil and mint leaves. Blitz for children with a hand blender and serve 'whole' for adults with the lime wedges. Serves about 6.

Italian country soup

This soup can be blended as a food for stage-two weaning. Adults can add seasoning later if they feel the need. It is really tasty served with some soft bread for little ones and for adults, slices of chargrilled sourdough bread rubbed with fresh garlic and a drizzle of extra virgin olive oil.

1 large onion, peeled and finely chopped
3 sticks celery, chopped
2 large carrots, peeled and chopped
2 cloves garlic, peeled
3 tbsp light olive oil
1 bay leaf
2 large King Edward potatoes, peeled and cut into 'stock cube'-size pieces
2 glasses dry white wine (if you decide to make an adults only version one day!)

½ small white cabbage

1 small pointed spring cabbage, outer leaves discarded, cored and cut lengthways

150g spring greens

1½l vegetable or chicken stock (page 181)

salt and black pepper

150g canned cannellini beans, drained and rinsed

200g butter beans, drained and rinsed

1 small bag baby-leaf spinach, rinsed

1 tsp Parmesan cheese (per person), grated

Finely chop the onions, and chop celery and carrots into chunkier pieces. Peel the garlic cloves. Heat olive oil in a large saucepan and add the chopped vegetables plus the bay leaf. Sauté over a medium to low heat for 20 minutes until ingredients are golden. Add cubed potatoes and turn heat up to medium, stirring all the while. Add the white wine and bring to the boil. Turn heat down to medium/low so it keeps simmering briskly. Meanwhile roughly chop the remaining green vegetables minus the spinach. Once the wine in the saucepan has reduced by half its volume, add the stock and the green vegetables. Bring to the boil then reduce heat and allow to simmer. Season with a little salt and black pepper to taste. Simmer gently, with the lid slightly askew, for 45 minutes. Add the cannellini and butter beans. Simmer for a further 45 minutes with the lid off. Finally, add the spinach. Stir well and serve with some freshly-grated Parmesan. Serves 6 adults.

Great because:

✓ *This is a really nourishing soup, providing energy-boosting iron and zinc to help your immune system.*

✓ *It is great too for beta carotene, the orange pigment in carrots, which may help protect our skin against sun damage and protects our lungs from air pollution.*

✓ *It provides a non-dairy way of getting the mineral calcium from the dark green vegetables, which helps to build and maintain strong bones.*

PASTA AND PIZZA *

Ricotta and tomato pasta

This dish is great served with some of your children's favourite vegetables on the side, or blended, or with some crunchy iceberg lettuce drizzled with Balsamic glaze. It is suitable from stage two of weaning, or for younger babies, if blended.

> 2 handfuls pasta
> 2 tbsp tomato sauce (page 183)
> 1 tbsp ricotta cheese
> 2 tsp Parmesan cheese, grated

Cook the pasta ('farfalle' butterfly shapes or 'fusilli' twirls work well) following pack instructions. Mix in enough tomato sauce to nicely coat the pasta. Stir in about 1 tbsp ricotta cheese per person. Grate over some Parmesan cheese before serving. Serves 1.

Courgette and tomato pasta

Suitable from stage-two weaning onwards. Serve with iceberg lettuce drizzled with Balsamic glaze.

> ½ medium-sized courgette, sliced into 'matchsticks'
> 1 tbsp olive oil
> 1 small handful fresh basil (optional)
> 2 handfuls pasta
> 2 tbsp tomato sauce (page 183)
> 1 tbsp Parmesan cheese

Slice courgette lengthways then across to make neat matchsticks (allowing half a medium courgette per adult). Heat a tablespoon of olive oil and sauté quite briskly at a high heat so that the courgette does not absorb too much oil and until slightly brown. Add some chopped basil too if you like it. Drain and set aside. Cook the appropriate amount of pasta ('farfalle' or twirls work well), then mix in enough tomato sauce to nicely coat it. Add the courgettes and serve sprinkled with grated Parmesan cheese. Serves 1.

Tuna pasta

We serve this dish with a tomato and red onion salad drizzled with a little extra-virgin olive oil or Balsamic glaze.

2 handfuls fusilli pasta (twirls)
50g tuna (canned in olive oil), drained
2 tbsp tomato sauce (page 183)

Cook the appropriate amount of fusilli pasta twirls according to pack instructions. Allow about 50g of tuna (canned in olive oil) per person. Open and drain the can. Gently break up the tuna and mix into the tomato sauce. Stir the sauce into the pasta. Serves 1.

Black olive and anchovy pasta

This is a children's version of 'Puttanesca' and is suitable for the over twos. For younger children, leave out the canned anchovies because they are too salty. Serve with iceberg lettuce drizzled with Balsamic glaze.

2 handfuls pasta (fusilli or farfalle)
2 black olives, chopped
½ canned anchovy, chopped
1 tbsp oil (from anchovy can)

½ **clove garlic**
2 tbsp tomato sauce (page 183)
1 large pinch parsley, chopped

Cook the pasta according to pack instructions, using an appropriate amount per person. Chop up 2 black olives per person and ½ a canned anchovy per adult and ¼ per child. Heat some of the oil from the anchovy can in a small pan. Add the olives and a tiny bit of crushed garlic. Next add the anchovies and stir. Pour in the tomato sauce and bring to the boil then simmer while you are cooking the pasta (10–12 minutes). Add some chopped parsley if you have it. Stir the sauce into the cooked pasta and serve. Serves 1.

Pasta salad

This can be blended for stage-two weaning but is probably best for children who are at the stage of eating chopped-up family meals.

2 handfuls pasta (fusilli or farfalle work well)
1 tsp olive oil
2 tbsp tomato sauce (page 183)
3 broccoli florets, chopped
1 tbsp frozen peas
1 tbsp chickpeas

Cook the appropriate amount of pasta per person, drain and cool, stirring in a little olive oil to keep it moist. Once cooled, stir in the tomato sauce so that the pasta is nicely coated and any cooked and cooled vegetables you and your children enjoy. Here I have suggested chopped broccoli florets, frozen peas (which you quickly cook and cool before adding), and some canned chickpeas (drained). Stir everything well and serve. Serves 1.

Salmon pasta

Suitable from stage-two weaning onwards. Serve with a tomato and red onion salad with Balsamic glaze.

2 handfuls pasta (shells work well)
2 tbsp tomato sauce (page 183)
50g salmon, cooked, deboned and flaked

Cook the appropriate amount of pasta per person (small shells work well), then mix in enough tomato sauce to nicely coat the pasta. Stir in about 50g of cooked, flaked salmon per person, checking carefully for bones before using. Serves 1.

Quick tip:

✓ *Cut off as much of the brown fat from the salmon as possible before cooking. Oily fish are known to contain pollutants. They accumulate in the flesh throughout the fish but especially in the obvious brown fat, which you sometimes see on the edges of fillets.*

Rigatoni al forno

Serve with iceberg lettuce with a Balsamic glaze.

500g rigatoni or other larger-sized pasta shapes
4–6 heaped tbsp tomato sauce
150g mozzarella cheese, cut into small pieces
1 tbsp Parmesan cheese
1 tbsp extra-virgin olive oil

Preheat the oven to 200°C/390°F/gas 6. Cook pasta according to pack instructions, drain and rinse, transfering to a shallow, oven-proof dish. Take about 4–6 heaped tbsp tomato sauce, spoon over the pasta and mix it in. Dot over ¾ of the chopped mozzarella and grate over about a tablespoon of Parmesan cheese to taste. Mix again. Drizzle over some olive oil, enough so that the top of the pasta slightly glistens. Bake in the oven for 20 minutes until the top starts to get crusty. Remove from oven and stir. Dot over remaining mozzarella and bake for a further 20 minutes. Serves 4.

Fusilli Pasta Twirls

This is suitable from stage-two weaning onwards although leave out the Parmesan until babies are one year old. As you are serving the ratatouille alongside pasta, leave out the potatoes in the ratatouille recipe. Serve with iceberg lettuce salad drizzled with Balsamic glaze.

> **2 handfuls fusilli pasta (twirls)**
> **2 tbsp ratatouille (page 230)**
> **1 tsp Parmesan cheese, grated**

Cook the pasta, following pack instructions, then drain, keeping a little of the water. Put the drained pasta back into the cooking pan and add a little bit of the drained water to make the pasta moist. Stir in 2 tbsp ratatouille. Serve topped with grated Parmesan. Serves 1.

TRADITIONAL PIZZAS

Suitable for children who can cope with chewing a pizza base. I feel absolutely no shame in buying ready-made pizza bases and keeping them in the freezer. However, that said, there is something incredibly nice about making your own dough if you have the time and the inclination. If the idea does not grab you, though, there is a quick ciabatta pizza recipe on page 198.

Pizza dough
• • • • • • • • • • •

500g strong plain white flour (ideally Tipo 00 flour)
325ml warm boiled water
3½g (½ sachet) dried bread-making yeast
½ tsp sugar
1 tsp salt
1 tbsp extra-virgin olive oil

Put the water, sugar and yeast into a large bowl and whisk together for a minute. Through a sieve add half of the flour, stirring with a wooden spoon. Add salt. Sieve in remaining flour stirring with your hand and pour in the olive oil. Lightly flour a mixing oil. Knead mixture until you have a soft dough. Lightly flour the mixing bowl of a food processor. Ensure the hook of the processor is properly attached. Add dough and knead for 5 minutes on the lowest setting. Alternatively knead by hand for 10 minutes. In either case do not over-knead. It is ready once it springs instantly back after pressing a finger in. Remove dough and divide into 5 dough balls. Place on a lightly floured tray and cover with a damp tea towel. Leave in a warm place for 3 hours to rise.
Roll each ball thinly to fit on to a 10in pizza tray. Makes 5 pizzas (9in).

Tip:

✓ *Dough balls can be frozen once they have risen and defrosted in an hour to make a quick and healthy pizza meal.*

✓ *This dough can also be used as a great general recipe for making bread.*

Pizza toppings:

Ricotta and Parma ham

> **1 pizza base (see above)**
> **1 tbsp tomato sauce (page 183)**
> **2 slices Parma ham**
> **50g ricotta**
> **1 tsp olive oil**

Spread the pizza base with tomato sauce. Cook in a preheated oven at 200°C/390°F/gas 6 for 3 minutes. Remove and top with 2 slices of Parma ham, 50g of crumbled ricotta cheese and a drizzle of olive oil. Return to oven for 5–10 minutes until the edges are golden. Remove and top with chopped rocket leaves for adults and older children if they like them, and serve. Serves 1.

Mozzarella and olives

> **1 pizza base (see above)**
> **1 tbsp tomato sauce (page 183)**
> **4 black olives**
> **40g mozzarella, chopped**

Spread pizza base with tomato sauce. Arrange 4 whole black olives and 40g chopped mozzarella over the pizza. Cook in a preheated oven, 200°C/390°F/gas 6, for 5–10 minutes until edges are golden-brown. Serves 1.

Roasted vegetables

> **1 pizza base (see above)**
> **1 tbsp tomato sauce (page 183)**
> **½ small courgette, roasted and in strips**
> **4 tomatoes, roasted**
> **1–2 slices aubergine, roasted and cut up**
> **1 tbsp cheddar, grated**

Spread the pizza base with tomato sauce and lay some strips of roasted vegetables on top. These can be anything from roasted tomatoes and strips of courgettes to pieces of aubergine. Top with some grated cheddar and cook in a preheated oven, 200°C/390°F/gas 6, for 5–10 minutes until edges are golden-brown. Serves 1.

Great because:

✓ *Many ready-made and takeaway pizzas pack in a lot of fat, including artery-clogging saturated fats. These traditional Italian-style thin pizzas are less calorific (about 500–600 calories each) and are light on saturated fats.*

✓ *The tomato base is packed with health-protective lycopene, the red antioxidant super-nutrient in tomatoes, which appears to help to protect our skin against sun damage (and is good for prostate health in boys and men).*

Quick ciabatta pizza

Suitable for children old enough to chew the ciabatta bread. As well as the toppings suggested below, you can invent other ciabatta pizzas with your children, adding new ingredients as they get older and their palette develops. Try gradually introducing things like anchovies and tiny bits of black olives. You may be surprised how much they take to these although use in moderation and watch salt in other foods on the days you do because both of these are naturally salty foods. You can try drizzling over a little olive oil or Balsamic glaze once the ciabatta pizzas are cooked.

For the ciabatta base:
> **1 ciabatta loaf, sliced lengthways**
> **2 tsp olive oil**
> **1 clove garlic, peeled**
> **1–2 tsp tomato sauce (page 183)**

Put a griddle pan on the hob on a high heat. Slice the loaf in half lengthways, drizzle over a little olive oil, then rub with the clove of garlic (this is optional but worth trying for small children to introduce them to the flavour). Lay the ciabatta, cut side up on the griddle. Keep it there for a few minutes until the griddle pan lines are well-marked (brown not black) on the bread. Remove. Spread on 1–2 tsp tomato sauce. Serves 4.

Options for the topping:

1. Slices of tomato, basil or flat-leaf parsley and 2 slices mozzarella cheese.

2. Thin slices of cooked potato with some fresh rosemary and crumbled mozzarella.

3. Slices of tomato with strips of grilled chicken and Parmesan cheese.

4. Slices of tomato, strips of ham and mozzarella.

5. Slices of tomato, basil leaves, a sprinkling of ricotta cheese and some shavings of Parmesan.

FISH *

Cod in Parma ham

. . . .

If you remove the Parma ham beforehand, you can blend the fish, ratatouille and potatoes and serve from stage-two weaning onwards. I would also remove the ham (and eat most of it myself!) until children are two years old because it is quite salty. At this stage, just give them a small piece. The fish will have taken on some of its flavour anyway and will taste delicious.

> **50–100g cod fillet or steak**
> **1 piece Parma ham (per cod fillet)**
> **2 tsp olive oil**
> **1 tbsp ratatouille (page 230)**

Wrap each piece of cod in the Parma ham. Wrap in cling film and put in the fridge for at least 60 minutes. This helps to keep the fish and ham together when you cook it. Preheat the oven to 200°C/390°F/gas 6. In a pan, heat the oil and add the fish wrapped in ham. Cook on each side until the Parma ham is crisp. Place on a baking tray and bake for 10 minutes. This will have the effect of steaming the fish for a fabulously delicate flavour. Serve with new boiled potatoes, noodles or rice and ratatouille.

Salmon parcel

. . . .

This baked fish is lovely served with mashed sweet potato and courgettes (or another favourite green vegetable).

> **2 tsp olive oil**
> **1 x 80g salmon fillet, skinned**
> **1 small pinch herb salt**
> **1 small pinch black pepper**

2 tsp fresh lemon juice
150g sweet potato, peeled and cut into 5 chunks
1 tbsp spring onion, chopped
1 tbsp fresh parsley, chopped
Courgettes or green vegetables of choice.

Preheat your oven to 180°C/350°F/gas 4. Brush a large piece of foil lightly with oil and place the fish in the centre. Season with salt, freshly ground pepper, and lemon juice. Fold up the foil to make a loose parcel. Bake for approximately 20–30 minutes or until the fish is cooked. While the fish is cooking, boil the peeled sweet potato chunks for 15–20 minutes until cooked. Drain and mash with 1tsp extra virgin olive oil, 1 tbsp chopped spring onion and 1 tbsp chopped parsley. Serve with courgettes or green vegetables of choice. Serves 1.

Fish Pie
· · · · · · · ·

Fish pie is a staple in many houses. The good thing is that you can play around with the types of fish you use once you have the basic recipe under your belt. It is suitable from one year onwards. Blitz or mash as appropriate for your little ones and serve with your favourite steamed or boiled vegetables.

4 large potatoes, peeled and cut into chunks
1 large onion, peeled and chopped
2 tbsp olive oil
250g pollock or cod, cut into chunks, bones removed
250g fresh salmon fillet, cut into chunks, bones removed
25g plain flour
300ml semi-skimmed milk
1 knob butter
1 splash semi-skimmed milk
50g strong cheddar
1 pinch herb salt

Preheat oven to 200°C/390°F/gas 6. Peel and chop potatoes and put in a pan of water to boil. Once cooked, drain, put back in the pan and mash with some semi-skimmed milk and a little butter. Put the lid on and put to one side. Peel and chop the onion. Add oil to a pan and cook for 15 minutes on a very low heat until soft. Stir in the flour and add a third of the milk. Stir constantly until it thickens. Remove from the heat and stir in the next third. Keep stirring until it thickens again. Pour in the final milk and put back on the heat, stirring constantly until a smooth white sauce has formed. Add a pinch of herb salt to season. Cut up the fish into smallish pieces and add to the sauce. Cook for around 6 minutes. Put the mix in a large ovenproof dish and top with the mashed potato. Cook for 20 minutes and then top with the cheese. Return to the oven and cook for a further 10 minutes. Serves 4.

Quick tip:

✓ *You can use sweet potato for the topping if you prefer and use all white fish if you don't want to include salmon. Sometimes I add peas and sweetcorn to the dish, when adding the fish, or some finely chopped cooked carrots to up the vegetable content and give a bit of extra colour.*

Lemon sole fillets

This dish is suitable from stage-two weaning onwards but you need to be really sure that all the bones have been removed before you blend.

1 fillet lemon sole (or other white flat fish), skinless and boned
1 tbsp flour, lightly seasoned with salt
1 small knob butter
1½ tbsp olive oil
1 fresh lemon, juiced
2tbsp water
1 handful flat-leafed parsley

Cut the fillet in half lengthways and coat in seasoned flour, dusting off the excess as you lift it out. Put the butter and oil in a frying pan and wait until they are sizzling. Add the fillets, using a spatula to flatten them down. Sauté for 1 minute each side. Remove fish and squeeze over lots of fresh lemon juice. Put the pan back on the heat and add 2 tbsp water. Bring to the boil, stirring all the time. Add a handful of chopped flat-leafed parsley, then pour over the fillet and serve. Serves 1.

Serve with:

- crushed new potatoes, which can be blended for babies

- a crisp iceberg-lettuce salad drizzled with Balsamic glaze for older children and adults; or some blended cooked vegetables for weaning babies.

Quick haddock

This simple dish works really well with new potatoes and steamed spring greens or cabbage.

150g haddock
1 pinch herb salt
1 pinch black pepper
100ml skimmed milk
150g new potatoes
1 tbsp pesto

Put 150g of haddock into a saucepan with the herb salt. Pour over 100ml of skimmed milk. Heat until almost boiling. Reduce heat, simmer for 15 minutes and serve with 150g of boiled new potatoes in their skins mixed with a tablespoon of pesto sauce. Serves 1.

Salmon and potato salad

· · · · · · · · · · · · · · · · · ·

Suitable for children who can cope with chopped family meals.

150g new potatoes, cooked and cut into quarters
1 spring onion, finely chopped
100g fresh cooked salmon (or canned red salmon), bones and skin
    removed
1 tbsp white wine vinegar
2–3 tbsp olive oil
1 small pinch salt
1 handful parsley, finely chopped

In a large bowl, combine the potatoes, spring onion and salmon. In a small bowl, whisk the vinegar and olive oil and a tiny pinch of salt (omit for under ones). When really well combined, add 2 tsp of the parsley to the fish and taste, adding more if you need to. Cover with clingflim, keep in the fridge and use when ready. Serves 1.

Great because:

✓ *Oily fish supplies the body with important omega 3 essential fats, needed for brain development.*

Rice 'n' fish cakes

150g sweet potatoes, peeled and chopped
2 tsp olive oil
½ medium onion, peeled and chopped
½ tsp ground cumin (optional)
½ tsp ground coriander (optional)
1 pinch ground mace
80g canned pink salmon, drained
large pinch fresh coriander, chopped
1 small bunch chives, chopped
few drops of Tabasco (optional)
2 tbsp cooked basmati rice
1 pinch herb salt
1 pinch black pepper

Boil sweet potatoes until soft (about 15–20 mins). Meanwhile heat a non-stick pan and brush lightly with oil. Cook onion with ground cumin, coriander and mace until soft. Add drained tinned salmon and remove from heat. Drain sweet potatoes when cooked and using a fork crush them and combine with salmon mixture. Combine coriander, chives and Tabasco (optional) with the basmati rice. Add to sweet potato mixture. Season with herb salt and pepper. The mixture should be firm enough to mould into little cake shapes or you can make one large fishcake. Using a non-stick frying pan, add a little oil, and cook the fishcakes on a moderate heat for 2–3 minutes each side. When potato cakes are lightly coloured, serve with your favourite vegetables. Serves 1.

MEAT ✳

Meatloaf
· · · · · · · · · ·

A lovely winter or summer dish as it can be served hot or cold, with seasonal vegetables or a green salad.

- 400g extra-lean minced beef
- 100g wholemeal breadcrumbs
- 1 small onion, finely chopped
- 1 stick celery, finely chopped
- 1 tbsp tomato ketchup
- 1 size 3 egg, beaten
- 1 pinch herb salt
- 1 pinch black pepper
- 1 pinch dried mixed herbs

Preheat oven to 180°C/350°F/gas 4. Mix all the ingredients together until well combined. Place in a lightly greased 450g loaf tin. Press down well, cover with foil and bake for 30 minutes. Take out of oven and drain off any excess fat, re-cover with foil and return to the oven for a further 30 minutes. Slice to serve. Serves 4.

Traditional Bolognese sauce

· ·

Here is another classic Italian recipe. A real labour of love, this sauce takes four hours to cook so it's worth making a big batch, putting some aside for the freezer. It blends well to form the base of later-stage weaning food, which can be combined with things like mashed potato, small pasta stars or couscous. Bolognese sauce can be served with spaghetti or used to make lasagne, to stuff pancakes or even to make a shepherd's pie.

3 tbsp olive oil
1 large onion, peeled and finely chopped
2 celery sticks, finely chopped
2 carrots, peeled and finely chopped
250g good-quality lean minced beef
250g good-quality lean minced pork (you can use all beef if you prefer)
350ml semi-skimmed milk
1 tsp nutmeg, grated
2 x 500ml bottles passata (sieved tomatoes)
500ml water
1 pinch salt

In a large wide saucepan put 3 tbsp olive oil and add the onion, celery and carrots and very gently sauté over a medium heat. You want all the vegetables to soften, which can take 20–30 minutes. Once soft, add the meat, stir in well and cook for 30–40 minutes (with no lid). This is a crucial part of making the Bolognese: you must give the meat time for the water in it to evaporate. Next, add the milk and allow to reduce for around 40 minutes on a lowish heat until, again, any liquid has almost evaporated. Now grate in a little nutmeg and add the passata. Now half-fill each passata bottle with water and add to the Bolognese. Put the lid on the pan, setting it slightly askew, and bring to the boil on a medium heat. Remove the lid, season with a little salt and then leave it to simmer, lid still askew, on the lowest heat possible for about 45 minutes. Take the lid off, stir and simmer for another 30 minutes. You know it is ready when it starts to pop. Serves 8.

Rice noodle stir-fry

*This dish is suitable for older children and is easier to eat
if you chop up the noodles once drained.*

50 rice noodles (raw weight)
2 tbsp white wine vinegar
1 tbsp granulated fruit sugar
1 red chilli, de-seeded and chopped (optional)
2 tsp olive oil
55g pork escalope, cut into thin strips
150g mushrooms, sliced
2 spring onions, sliced
60g mangetout peas
1 carrot, peeled and grated
1 tsp reduced-salt soy sauce
150g beansprouts
1 tbsp fresh coriander, chopped

Prepare noodles as per the pack instructions. Mix vinegar, sugar and chilli (optional)
in a small pan and bring to the boil. Heat a non-stick frying pan and brush with a
little oil. When the pan is hot add pork strips and cook thoroughly. Place cooked pork
on absorbent paper and clean pan. Return pan to stove and add a little more oil to
the pan, then throw in mushrooms, sliced onions, mangetouts and grated carrot. Let
the vegetables cook for a couple of minutes and then add soy sauce and beansprouts.
Cook for a further minute, then add drained rice noodles. Mix coriander with vinegar
and chilli mixture. Mix noodles well into stir-fry and serve with sauce drizzled over.
Serves 1.

Cottage pie with carrots and peas

200g sweet potatoes, peeled and cut up
1 tbsp olive oil
100g extra-lean minced beef (or lamb)
½ onion, peeled and finely chopped
60g button mushrooms, sliced
1 clove garlic, peeled and crushed
½ tbsp tomato purée
1 tsp plain flour
1 tbsp homemade tomato sauce (page 183)
100ml homemade stock (or use low-salt stock cube)
1 pinch herb salt (page 180)
1 pinch black pepper
200ml skimmed milk
1 tsp mild horseradish relish or Dijon mustard (optional)
½ tsp nutmeg, grated
1 portion of peas & carrots, cooked

Boil sweet potatoes in salted water for 12–15 minutes. Meanwhile, heat oil in a non-stick frying pan on a moderate heat. Add minced beef and allow the meat to brown. Add chopped onion, mushrooms & garlic and cook until vegetables are soft. Then add tomato purée, flour, tomato sauce and stock. Let the mixture simmer for about 10–12 minutes and season to taste. Once the potatoes are cooked drain them and mash with the skimmed milk, horseradish relish (optional) and nutmeg till smooth & fluffy and leave to one side. Preheat grill to maximum. Place cooked meat mixture in a small, flat casserole dish and top with the mashed potato. Put the cottage pie under the grill for 6–8 minutes to lightly brown and serve with cooked peas and carrots. Serves 2.

Basic mince

Once you have cooked this mince there are plenty of dishes you can make from it, not least of course, shepherd's pie.

1 tbsp olive oil
1 small onion, peeled and chopped
1 small carrot, peeled and chopped
1 stick celery, chopped
250g extra-lean minced beef
1 tbsp oatmeal
150ml homemade stock (page 181)
1 pinch herb salt
1 tsp homemade tomato sauce (page 183)
1 large pinch fresh parsley, chopped

Heat the oil in a pan and gently cook the onion, carrots and celery until soft. Do not allow to go brown. It should take about 15 minutes stirring regularly. Remove and set aside. Add the beef to the pan and cook quickly, stirring it all the while so that it browns completely. Add back the onion mix and the oatmeal and then the stock and a pinch of herb salt and the tomato sauce. Simmer very slowly with a lid on for 1 hour or until tender. The sauce should not boil and will need stirring from time to time so that it does not stick. Taste and add some fresh chopped parsley and more homemade tomato sauce if you need to. It is now ready to freeze or use. Serves 2.

A perfect steak

It may seem odd to include a steak in a book about cooking for children. But they can enjoy it if prepared correctly. Small, lean and tender pieces of steak are actually not difficult to eat and can be blended for little ones. Good quality steak literally melts in the mouth when cooked to perfection. Serve with sautéed broccoli with garlic (page 234) and oven chips.

2 x 225g fillet steaks, good quality and 1cm thick
1 tbsp olive oil
1 pinch salt (per adult's steak)
1 tsp coarsely ground black pepper (adults)

Put steak on a plate and brush with olive oil so that it is lightly coated. Take griddle pan and brush with oil. Get it very hot on the hob then turn heat to medium. Quickly put steak on griddle pan and leave for 15 seconds then turn. It shouldn't stick but be careful in case it does. Cook for another 15 seconds. Remove and leave to rest for a few minutes. Season before serving for adults. Serves 2.

Great because:

✓ *Steak is highly nutritious, providing easily-absorbed iron for energy and zinc for strong immunity.*

Sausages with spring onion mash

200g sweet potatoes, peeled and chopped
2 Quorn sausages
1 small head broccoli florets
1 splash semi-skimmed milk
4 spring onions, finely chopped
1 pinch pepper

Boil sweet potatoes for 15–20 minutes. While they are cooking grill the sausages. While these are cooking prepare and cook broccoli, tearing off the florets. When potatoes are cooked, drain and mash with semi-skimmed milk until smooth. Beat spring onions into the mash and add seasoning to taste. Serve mash topped with sausages and broccoli on the side. Serves 1.

Shepherd's pie

This is suitable for children of one year or more. Peas always make a popular accompaniment.

>**1 double-sized batch of basic mince (see above)**
>**500g potatoes, peeled and chopped**
>**1 splash milk**

Make up the basic mince recipe but allow to simmer for longer until more of the liquid has evaporated and the mince is firmer. (Alternatively, use half of the stock when making the mince.) Cook the potatoes in boiling water for about 20 minutes until soft, then drain and mash with the milk. Put the mince into a non-stick 600ml pie dish (or 4 individual-size pie dishes), then spread the mash evenly on top. Run a fork across the top and brush lightly with milk. Bake in a preheated oven at 220°C/430°F/gas 7 for 30 minutes to brown the pie. The shepherd's pie can then be served or frozen. Serves 4.

Lamb cutlets with garlic and rosemary

Most suitable for children who can cope with chopped family meals although small pieces of lamb and ratatouille can easily be blended for younger children from stage-two weaning onwards.

>**3 lamb cutlets**
>**3 tbsp olive oil**
>**1 clove garlic, chopped**
>**1 sprig rosemary, destalked and finely chopped**
>**1 tsp lemon juice**
>**2 tbsp ratatouille (page 230)**
>**1 slice ciabatta bread**

Put lamb cutlets in a bowl with olive oil, chopped garlic and rosemary. Mix together and leave to marinade for 30 minutes if you have time. Get a griddle pan hot, then turn the heat down to medium. Cook the cutlets to your taste. 4 minutes each side is a good guide. Add a little lemon juice and serve with ratatouille and some ciabatta bread, which you cut into slices and put on the griddle pan (clean off any bits of burned cutlet first). Leave for a few minutes to create a nice crunchy bruschetta. Rub with garlic and serve with the cutlets. Serves 1.

Lamb with star anise

A slow-cooker recipe, suitable from stage-two weaning onwards. The slow cooking allows the fat from the lamb to melt away into the onions leaving a leaner, healthier meat to serve.

> **3 tbsp olive oil**
> **1 shoulder of lamb, visible fat removed**
> **3 large onions, peeled and sliced**
> **3 star anise**
> **150ml water**

Heat oil in a large non-stick frying pan on a medium heat. Add the lamb and brown on all sides. This will take 15–20 minutes. Place onions in the slow cooker and arrange the star anise among the onions. Add the water. Put the lamb on top of the onions and close. Set the dial to low and leave for 6–8 hours. Remove lamb, pour juices into a frying pan and briskly bubble to reduce volume to about a third. Carve the lamb and serve with the reduced juices as sauce. This dish is lovely served with roasted vegetables (page 232). Serves 6.

Great because:

✓ *The lamb gives us: selenium, a trace mineral that is vital for a healthy immune system and*

  heart; and iron, the mineral needed for energy and good concentration.

Pork stir-fry

Suitable for older children who like to be a little adventurous.

100g extra-lean pork, cut into small cubes
1 tbsp fresh orange juice
1 tsp reduced-salt soy sauce
1 tsp white wine vinegar
½ clove garlic, peeled and sliced
2 tsp olive oil
125g frozen stir-fry mixed vegetables
50ml vegetable stock (or use homemade: page 181)
1 tsp honey
1 tsp cornflour
1 pinch salt
1 pinch black pepper
60g basmati rice, cooked

Place pork in a shallow dish. Whisk together orange juice, soy sauce and wine vinegar, adding the sliced garlic and pour over the pork pieces. Cover and marinate for 1 hour. Strain, reserving the marinade. Brush a non-stick frying pan very lightly with oil and, when hot, add pork and stir-fry for 5 minutes or until well-cooked. Remove with a slotted spoon and set aside. Brush pan again with a little oil and add the frozen stir-fry mixed vegetables and fry for 5 minutes or until cooked. Return the pork to the pan. Mix reserved marinade with the stock, honey and cornflour and stir into the vegetables and pork. Cover the pan and simmer for 2–3 minutes. Season with salt and pepper and serve at once with the basmati rice. Serves 1.

POULTRY *

Chicken and vegetable hotpot

* *

This winter-warmer is lovely when served with a baked sweet potato on the side.
You can blend this meal for a child of over one.

1 tbsp oil
1 x 100g chicken breast, skinless
2 celery sticks, chopped
2 carrots, peeled and sliced
1 onion, peeled and sliced
¼pt stock (page 181)
thyme
1 pinch herb salt (page 180)
1 pinch black pepper
150g sweet potato
1 tbsp half-fat crème fraiche

Add a tablespoon of olive oil to a medium-sized pan and heat. Add the celery, carrots and onions and sauté for 10 minutes. Two minutes before this cooking time is up, add a crushed clove of garlic. Pour in your homemade chicken stock. Add a small sprig of thyme and a tiny pinch of herb salt and black pepper to taste. Bring to the boil and then simmer for 30 minutes. Brush a non-stick pan with olive oil and add the chicken breast and sauté each side until cooked through. Remove from the pan and set aside. Once cooled slightly, cut into chunks. Remove vegetable stock from heat and blitz lightly with a hand-held food blender. Add the chopped chicken and serve in a bowl with a whirl of crème fraiche. Serves 1.

Mashed potatoes with chicken

This is a really nice way to serve potatoes from babies onwards. It can be blended and is suitable from stage two of weaning.

1 baking potato (or ½, depending on age)
1 tsp olive oil
100g cooked chicken, chopped
1 tbsp tomato sauce
1 spring onion, chopped finely (optional)

Bake a potato as you normally would in the microwave or oven (see page 173). Once cooked, cut in half and scoop out the soft flesh and mash with the olive oil. Then pass the potato through a ricer (or blitz with a hand blender). This gives a really smooth mash, which children find easy to eat. Next, take some cooked lean chicken and cut into bite-sized pieces and mix with 1 tbsp tomato sauce. Blend if you need to. Put the mash in a bowl, make a little nest for the sauce and garnish with some finely chopped spring onion (optional). Serve with some favourite vegetables. Serves 1.

Roasted rosemary chicken thighs

You can remove the cooked chicken meat from the bone, discard the skin and blend this for a weaning meal or cut up into small pieces for older children. Suitable from stage-two weaning onwards.

1–2 chicken thighs
1 tbsp olive oil
1 sprig fresh rosemary
1 clove fresh garlic, peeled
1–2 tbsp ratatouille (page 230)
2 new potatoes, washed

Put the chicken thighs into a bowl, rub with little olive oil, sprinkle over a few rosemary needles and add the whole clove of peeled garlic. Drizzle over a little extra olive oil and set aside in the fridge. When ready to cook, put in the oven, preheated to 180°C/350°F/gas 4, for 45–50 minutes. They are ready when the meat falls off the bone. Serve with the ratatouille and some new boiled potatoes. Serves 1.

Turkey kebabs in pitta bread

This is only suitable for older children, once fully weaned, when they can cope with chunks of meat and pitta.

¼ onion, layers separated
100g turkey, cubed
½ green pepper, deseeded and cut into squares
6 cherry tomatoes
1 tsp olive oil
1 small wholemeal pitta bread
1 tablespoon of tzatsiki

Separate each layer of the onion then thread each piece onto a skewer with cubes of the turkey, green pepper and cherry tomato alternately. Brush very lightly with oil. Place either over a barbecue or under a grill until the turkey is cooked through. Warm the pitta, and slit . Unthread the cooked turkey and vegetables, stuffing them into the pitta pocket and serve with tzatsiki. (If you don't want to buy ready-made, you can make your own tzatsiki by mixing grated cucumber with some low-fat plain yoghurt and a little cayenne pepper.) Serves 1.

Sautéed chicken breasts with potato and peas

When weaning, you can blend the chicken in tomato sauce (page 183) with the peas and a little cooked boiled potato. Only give the mozzarella to children over one.

> 1 potato, peeled and cut into small cubes
> 1 tbsp olive oil
> 1 chicken breast
> 150ml stock (page 181)
> 1 tbsp tomato sauce (page 183)
> 1 slice mozzarella cheese
> 1 garlic clove, peeled and chopped
> 1–2 tbsp frozen peas

Preheat oven to 180°C/350°F/gas 4. Spread the potato cubes in the bottom of a roasting tin, sprinkle over olive oil so that they are lightly coated and roast for 40 minutes. Sauté the chicken breast gently in saucepan with a little olive oil until browned and the juices run clear when you pierce. Remove from the pan and cover with foil. Put the stock in the pan and boil until it reduces by two-thirds. Add a tablespoon of tomato sauce and once it starts bubbling, place the sauce and chicken breast in a grill-pan. Make sure the breast is totally coated by the sauce. Place a slice of mozzarella on top of the chicken and place under the grill for 15 seconds. (If preparing for a weaning diet, miss this step out.) Put the chicken on a plate and if the sauce is runny, reduce a bit in the pan. Pour the sauce over the chicken. Add a little olive oil to the saucepan, then a garlic clove, peeled and chopped in half. Turn the heat up and get the garlic browned. Then throw in the frozen peas. Stir until the ice-water has evaporated and the peas are soft. This takes about 5 minutes. Serve with the roasted potato cubes. Serves 1.

Chicken cacciatore

. . . .

If you remove the skin from the chicken once cooked and blend, this is suitable from stage-two weaning onwards.

1 leg and thigh of chicken
1 potato, peeled and cut into pieces
1 carrot, peeled and chopped
1 large tomato, cored and cut into 8
1 red onion, peeled and cut into quarters
1 sprig fresh rosemary (or 1 pinch dried)
1 pinch thyme
2 tsp olive oil
1 tbsp stock (page 181)
2 new potatoes, boiled
1 tbsp olive oil
2 tbsp maple syrup

Preheat oven to 180°C/350°F/gas 4. Put the chicken on a baking tray and place the vegetables around it. Next sprinkle on the herbs. Drizzle over the olive oil and 1 tbsp stock. Roast in the oven for 45 minutes to 1 hour until when the chicken is pierced its juices run clear. Serve with new boiled potatoes which, after cooking and draining, you put in a pan with hot olive oil and toss for a few minutes. For a real treat, add 2 tbsp maple syrup. Serves 1.

Roasted rosemary chicken thighs with croutons

You can prepare the chicken thighs in the morning and then cook them later. They make a great finger food and help to introduce children to herbs. You can remove the cooked chicken meat from the bone, discard the skin and blend this for a weaning meal or cut up into small pieces for older children.

2 chicken thighs (or 1 per child)
1 tbsp olive oil
1 pinch fresh rosemary
1 clove fresh garlic, peeled
1 slice ciabatta bread, chopped into small cubes
1 portion of roasted vegetables (page 232)

Preheat oven to 180°C/350°F/gas 4. Put the chicken thighs into a bowl, rub with a little olive oil and sprinkle over a few rosemary leaves. Add the whole clove of peeled garlic and the croutons. Season by drizzling over a little extra olive oil. Set aside in the fridge to marinate for 1 hour, if you can. Next put the chicken thighs in the oven for 45–50 minutes. They are ready when the meat can come away from the bone. Remove the skin when serving to the children. Older children can enjoy eating the meat from the bone but only allow this when you are supervising carefully. Serve with some roasted vegetables (page 232) or with other favourite vegetables. Serves 1.

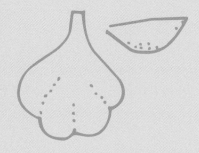

VEGETABLES *

Risotto

· · · · · · ·

Risotto is one of those dishes that many children and adults enjoy, depending of course what you put into it. It is also one of the dishes that makes great use of your tasty stock. There are two choices regarding the way to go about making your risotto: the longer and more traditional way and the quick way. Choose whichever suits you best. In terms of keeping leftover risotto: I have heard varying views on the safety of reheating rice. However, I would never reheat rice. If kept in the fridge it is fine to serve cold.

The traditional way:

> 1 medium–large onion, chopped roughly into small pieces
> 75g Italian arborio rice, per person
> extra-virgin olive oil
> 2 cloves garlic, minced (optional)
> 1l vegetable or chicken stock (page 181)
> 1 pinch salt
> 1 pinch freshly ground pepper
> 1 tbsp Parmesan cheese, grated
> 1 pinch saffron (optional)
> 1 large handful mushrooms, peeled and sliced (optional)
> 2 tbsp porcini mushrooms, dried (optional)

Fry onions in olive oil, until soft but not browned, in a large frying pan or deep pot. Add risotto rice and coat the rice grains thoroughly with olive oil. Add garlic if desired, (my children love it with garlic but it is not to everyone's taste). Add a splash of stock and stir until largely soaked up by the rice. Keep stirring the rice so that it doesn't stick to the bottom of the pan and add stock little by little as the rice absorbs it.

After about 15–20 minutes, when the rice is almost cooked and most of the stock has been absorbed, season with a tiny bit of salt and pepper. Add grated parmesan to taste. Serves 6.

Optional extras:

- saffron: adds colour and flavour to the risotto, which my children love. If you use saffron this should be added early in the cooking at the same time as the rice.

- mushrooms: I often make the risotto using a mixture of dried porcini and fresh mushrooms. You need to add a large handful of fresh, sliced mushrooms to the onions and fry them in the oil as well as soaking 2 tbsp dried porcini in boiling water (these are added to the rice when it is first mixed with the onions and before any stock is poured in). I then add the stock as normal and continue as above.

- vegetables: cut any vegetables you want to use into small chunks (pea-sized) and cook separately in salted boiling water. (A child's handful makes one portion.) Drain, keeping the water as stock for the risotto and set on one side. Make the plain risotto as above, using the vegetable water as part or your stock, then add the vegetables when the rice is almost cooked. I find that peas, carrots and asparagus all work well in a children's vegetable risotto.

As my children's daddy, Franco, says, this really is a 'twist' on risotto because it is not using the 'right' arborio rice and has none of the normal risotto method. The fact is, though, that it tastes good and can be served as a family dinner. It is suitable for the whole family and babies at stage-two weaning but you may need to blend a portion for a them, or partially blend it as they progress.

1 sachet Uncle Ben's boil-in-the-bag rice
1 tiny knob butter

Take a sachet of rice and cook as per pack instructions (1 sachet per adult). Transfer to a bowl adding butter.

Here is what you can then add:

Broccoli and chicken

1 handful small broccoli florets
1 tbsp olive oil
1 clove garlic, peeled and crushed
1 handful of cooked chicken, chopped

Boil the broccoli, breaking it into small florets first. When cooked through, transfer to a colander and place a saucepan lid over it. In the pan in which it was cooked, add the olive oil and garlic. Cook for 45 seconds, no longer, until the colour has just been taken off the garlic but it is not yet brown. Add back the broccoli (the water in the broccoli will stop the garlic from cooking any further), and keep stirring on a medium heat for 5–6 minutes. Next add the rice and stir it in. Then add the cooked chicken pieces. (If it has been boiled in your stock then it's fine to use as there's enough flavour in this dish to cover the fact that it is a little tasteless after so much boiling!). Serves 1. **Note:** instead of the chicken you could use: flakes of cooked salmon; or strips of cooked beef, lamb or pork (whatever leftover meat or fish you have in the fridge).

Hummus on toasted rye

Serve with lots of vegetable sticks: carrots, cucumber, peppers – whatever takes your fancy!

150g chickpeas, drained
½ lemon, juiced
1 tsp crunchy peanut butter (if allergic to nuts, omit)
1 tsp fresh mint, chopped
1 clove garlic, peeled and crushed
1 pinch black pepper (optional)
1 slice rye bread, toasted (per person)

Put 150g canned, drained chickpeas in a small blender or food processor and add the lemon juice, crunchy peanut butter and fresh mint. Blend until the ingredients start to break down. Add the garlic and continue to blend until a smooth paste starts to form. Season with pepper to taste. Meanwhile toast a slice of rye bread until crisp. Serve the hummus on the rye toast. Serves 1.

Spanish omelette

This is lovely served with an iceberg lettuce salad drizzled with Balsamic glaze and is best for children once fully weaned.

2 tsp olive oil
½ onion, finely chopped
½ green pepper, seeded and chopped
150g sweet potato, boiled and cubed
2 eggs, whisked in a bowl
1 pinch herb salt (page 180)
1 pinch black pepper

Brush a non-stick frying pan lightly with oil and gently fry onion and green pepper until soft. Add the cooked cubes of sweet potato and cook for about a minute. Beat the eggs and season with a little herb salt and ground black pepper. Pour into the frying pan. Allow to cook until the top looks cooked. Heat grill to high and finish omelette off under grill until the top is cooked. Turn out onto plate. Serves 1.

Sweet potato pie

This dish is lovely served with a green salad drizzled with balsamic glaze.

60g lean back bacon, rind removed
150g sweet potato
1 slice granary bread, crumbed
1 tbsp chives, chopped
1 tsp grain mustard
1 tsp Dijon mustard
1 shallot, finely chopped
1 pinch black pepper
1 bowl prepared mixed salad leaves
a little salad dressing

Preheat grill to maximum. Cook bacon under grill for 4–5 minutes. Wrap sweet potato in absorbent paper and microwave on high for 8 minutes. While bacon and sweet potato are cooking prepare the topping. Chop up the bread into medium-sized crumbs and mix with chives, mustards and finely chopped shallot. When bacon is cooked chop finely and mix with bread mixture. Take sweet potato out of oven when cooked, slice horizontally, season and then spoon on the bread and bacon topping. Place the sweet potato under the grill and cook until topping is well browned. Serve immediately. Serves 1.

Moroccan chickpea casserole with bulgur wheat

Most suitable for children once fully weaned. If giving to children under one, leave the salt out and blend appropriately. However, the spices might be a bit much for them if they are not used to spicy food.

2 tsp olive oil
½ medium onion, peeled and chopped
50g button mushrooms, finely sliced
1 clove garlic, peeled and crushed
90g chickpeas, drained
½ tsp ground cumin
½ tsp ground coriander
2 tsp tomato purée
100g chopped canned tomatoes
50g sultanas (soaked in 100ml boiling water)
550ml stock (page 181) (or use a low-salt vegetable stock cube)
6 tbsp bulgur wheat
1 tsp parsley, chopped
1 tiny pinch salt
1 small pinch cayenne pepper

Heat a moderate-sized saucepan and brush with a little oil. Add the onions and mushrooms and cook until soft. Add garlic, chickpeas, cumin and coriander and cook for about a minute. Add tomato purée, tinned tomatoes, sultanas (plus the water they were soaked in) and 250ml of the vegetable stock. Bring to the boil and turn down the heat to simmer gently for 10 minutes. Meanwhile put the bulgur wheat in a saucepan over a high heat and cook dry for 2–4 minutes. Pour on remaining 300ml of vegetable stock, turn off the heat and cover with a tight-fitting lid or foil and leave for 5–6 minutes or until all the stock has been absorbed. When the chickpeas are ready, remove from the heat, add parsley and season with salt and cayenne pepper to taste. Serve bulgur wheat and spoon chickpea casserole on top. Serves 1.

Pancakes with ricotta

This dish is very soft, but it most suitable for when you no longer need to purée your baby's food. Serve with a simple salad.

1 tbsp tomato sauce (page 183) per pancake
1 tbsp ricotta cheese per pancake
Few leaves baby spinach
1 egg
Little chopped mozzarella
125g self-raising flour
1 small pinch salt
1 egg
185ml milk
oil to brush frying pan

Mix ricotta in a bowl with a grating of Parmesan cheese and the spinach. Break in the egg and set aside. Sieve the flour into a bowl and add the salt. Make a 'well' in the middle and drop in the egg with half the milk. Begin mixing. When thick and creamy and all the flour has been beaten in, lightly stir in the rest of the milk. Heat a small non-stick frying pan and brush with oil. Pour over enough of the pancake mixture to thinly cover the base of the pan. Cook until the pancake is golden underneath, then toss and cook again until the second side puffs up. Spread each pancake with ricotta mix and roll up. Spoon over the tomato sauce and a little chopped mozzarella. Bake for 10 minutes at 180°C/350°F/gas 4. Serves 1. Makes 4 pancakes.

Bulgur wheat with apricots

Most suitable for children once fully weaned. If giving to children under one, bear in mind that the spices may be a bit much for them if not used to spicy food and definitely leave out the Tabasco.

2 tsp olive oil
50g bulgur wheat
½ onion, finely chopped
1 pinch ground cinnamon
25g raisins
50g dried apricots
300ml stock (page 181)
1 large packet fresh baby spinach leaves
1 bunch fresh basil leaves
50g cooked chickpeas
½ tsp chilli sauce or Tabasco sauce (optional)
½ lemon, zest and juice
½ tsp fresh nutmeg, grated

In a saucepan add a little oil, then the bulgur wheat and onion. Cook gently and add the cinnamon, raisins and dried apricots. When the ingredients are well-mixed add stock and turn the heat down to low. Cover with a lid and let the bulgur wheat absorb all the liquid, which should take about 6 minutes. Add a little of the spinach and all the basil leaves, together with the chickpeas, to the cooked bulgur wheat. Mix thoroughly and add chilli sauce (optional), lemon zest and juice. Steam or boil the rest of the spinach. Place cooked bulgur wheat on plate with cooked spinach and grate a little nutmeg for extra flavour. Serves 1.

Red kidney bean pulao

Most suitable for children once fully weaned. If giving to children under one, leave out the herb salt and blend appropriately. However, the spices might be a bit much if they're not not used to spicy food.

5 tbsp basmati rice
1 tsp olive oil
½ cinnamon stick
1 clove
2 green cardamom pods
½ onion, peeled and sliced
½ tsp ginger, freshly grated
1 pinch chilli powder
1 pinch turmeric
1 clove garlic, peeled and crushed
½ tsp garam masala
60g frozen peas
60g cauliflower florets
1 carrot, sliced
1 courgette, sliced
80g cooked red kidney beans
½ tbsp lemon juice
1 tbsp fresh coriander leaves, chopped
1 pinch herb salt (page 180)
300ml water

Wash the rice in cold water and leave to soak while you prepare the other ingredients. Heat a saucepan over a moderate heat and brush lightly with oil. Add cinnamon, cloves and cardamom and cook for about a minute. Add chopped onion and fry gently for 2 minutes. Add ginger, chilli powder and turmeric, garlic and garam masala, followed by the peas and cauliflower. Continue to cook gently and then add carrot and courgette. Drain the rice and put it, along with the kidney beans, into the pan with vegetables. Stir gently and then add the lemon juice, coriander, a little salt and the water. Bring to the boil, then turn down and cover with a lid. Leave for 12–15 minutes till all the water has been absorbed and the rice is cooked. Let the pulao settle for 5 minutes before serving. Serves 1.

Ratatouille

This is another wonderfully versatile dish from which you can make many others. I have given you Franco's grandma's version, which includes potatoes, but these need to be left out for some of the uses for ratatouille that include pasta, so read each of the recipes through quickly before making up your batch. Ratatouille is suitable for children from stage-two weaning onwards.

> 2 tbsp olive oil
> 1 medium–large red onion, peeled and chopped
> 1 clove garlic, peeled and crushed
> 2 large courgettes, sliced and chopped into cubes
> 1 potato, boiled (but firmish) and chopped into small cubes
> 4 large ripe tomatoes, cut in half with core removed
> 1 large aubergine, chopped into little cubes
> Runner beans, cut into diamond shapes (optional)

Heat 1 tbsp olive oil in a medium-sized pan and add the onions. Cook on a low-ish heat for about 10 minutes until soft but not browned. You need to keep stirring them to achieve this result. When almost soft, add the crushed garlic and stir again briefly. Remove the onions and garlic and set aside in a bowl. Add the aubergines and beans (if using) into the pan. You may need a little more oil (but try to resist unless really necessary because once you add the onions back, the vegetables absorb oil from them). Once softened, add back the onion and garlic, as well as the courgettes and tomatoes. Cook until the water in the tomatoes is reduced and they are nicely softened and broken down. If using potato, add at this point with 1 tbsp olive oil. The potatoes need to be nicely coated with the mix so that the tomatoes stick to them. It is now ready to serve or freeze. Serves 4.

Great because:

✓ *Ratatouille is a wonderful way of introducing all sorts of vegetables into a meal, from vitamin C-rich peppers (there is still some remaining even after cooking because there is so much in the first place) to aubergines, which have purple antioxidant super-nutrients in their skin.*

Five recipes that use ratatouille:

Lamb cutlets with garlic and rosemary (page 212)
Cod in Parma ham (page 200)
Roasted rosemary chicken thighs (page 216)
Fusilli pasta twirls (page 195)
Bruschetta (page 231)

Bruschetta

Suitable from when your child can cope with chewing the ciabatta. For second-stage weaning infants, serve the bean mix and ratatouille on a plate with some of their favourite cooked grains (e.g. couscous, rice or pasta) at an appropriate consistency.

2 tbsp olive oil
3 cloves garlic
Small sprig fresh rosemary
1 large can cannellini beans, drained and rinsed
200–250ml stock (page 181)

1 slice ciabatta bread (per person), sliced lengthways
1 tbsp ratatouille (per person) (page 230)

In a saucepan, heat 2 tbsp olive oil and gently cook the cloves of peeled garlic (which should be left whole). Once the garlic is browned, add the beans and mix in well. Put half of the mix into a blender and blitz with about 200–250ml stock. Blend until semi-crushed. Return bean mixture to the saucepan and simmer for 10 minutes. Meanwhile, slice the ciabatta in half lengthways and brush with olive oil. Cook on a griddle until crisp and nicely marked with griddle lines. Spread each piece of ciabatta with 1 tbsp ratatouille and top with the beans. Serves 2.

Roasted vegetables

Suitable for all ages and can be blended for weaning.

2 parsnips, peeled and sliced
2 carrots, peeled and sliced
2 red onions, peeled and cut in half
2 sweet potatoes, peeled and cut in half
1 Maris Piper potato, peeled and quartered
2 sprigs fresh rosemary
4 cloves garlic, unpeeled
3 tbsp extra-virgin olive oil
sea salt and black pepper

Preheat oven to 180°C/350°F/gas 4. Put all ingredients into a large roasting tin. Pour over the olive oil and mix with your hands. Season with a little sea salt and black pepper for the section of vegetables you intend to serve to adults. Roast in the oven for about 45 minutes and serve. Serves 4.

Sweet potato mash with fried egg

Suitable for children over one who are eating chopped family food. Serve with an iceberg lettuce salad drizzled with Balsamic glaze.

3 medium-sized sweet potatoes, peeled and evenly cubed
25ml olive oil
1 clove garlic, peeled and crushed
4 small eggs
1 green chilli, finely chopped (optional)
1 large bunch flat-leaf parsley, stems removed and finely chopped

Boil sweet potatoes for 15 minutes or until just cooked. Meanwhile gently heat 2 tsp olive oil in a very small pan. Add the garlic as the oil is heating. As soon as the garlic starts to go golden, remove immediately from the heat and set aside. When sweet potatoes are cooked, turn into a colander and drain. Put a lid on the colander to steam them dry. Put the remaining oil in a non-stick frying pan and fry the eggs (and separately, the optional chilli) then set aside. (Eggs must be cooked until hard for children.) Mash the sweet potatoes with a masher or hand blender. Add the garlic (plus the chilli if using) and the fried eggs, chopped into smallish pieces with a knife and fork. Add 90 per cent of the chopped parsley and mix again for a few seconds. Serve garnished with remaining parsley. Serves 2.

Great because:

✓ *Sweet potatoes are uniquely rich in three potent antioxidants: vitamin C, vitamin E, and beta carotene – which protect children's immunity and eye health.*

✓ *They are a low GI (glycaemic index) food, which means they are digested slowly and keep us feeling fuller for longer.*

✓ *Eggs are good for protein and provide a little vitamin D, needed to absorb bone-building calcium.*

Sautéed broccoli with garlic

Cooking broccoli this way can help tone down its bitter tones.

1 large head broccoli
3 tbsp extra-virgin olive oil
4 large cloves garlic, peeled and chopped in half

Chop the broccoli until florets are quite small then boil until properly cooked. Drain and put a lid on the colander to steam out any excess moisture. Take a frying pan and heat at least 3 tbsp extra-virgin olive oil. Add the garlic and fry until golden brown. Add the broccoli (be careful it may sizzle). Sauté well over a medium to high heat for 3–4 minutes. Turn heat down and carry on sautéing for a further 2–3 minutes. There should be no residue of water. It doesn't matter if the broccoli breaks down a bit. Serves 4.

Serving suggestions:

serve with the steak (page 210)

add a chopped canned anchovy and serve with lamb cutlets (page 212)

serve with any piece of grilled meat

stir into cooked pasta

put on top of toasted ciabatta bread, topped with a slice of mozzarella cheese, and grill

add to the quick risotto (page 221)

for adults, add 1 chopped and seeded fresh birds-eye green chilli to the garlic, while frying, and just before adding broccoli

Slow-cooked carrots

4 small carrots, cleaned and rinsed (peel and chop if larger-sized)
1 knob butter

Place carrots in a saucepan with a well-fitting lid. Add a good knob of butter. Put on the smallest ring and lowest heat and leave with the lid on for 20 minutes. Carrots will be soft, sweet and divine. Remove carrots from pan. Reduce the leftover juices a little and pour over carrots. Serves 2.

OMELETTES

Omelettes are another of those dishes that, once you have mastered, you can replicate time and again adding different ingredients to ring the changes. We serve our omelettes with cooked potato rather than bread. I prefer to keep salt-intake down that way and it means that I can season the omelette making it more appealing.

Herb omelette

3 medium-sized fresh eggs
1 tiny pinch salt
1 pinch freshly ground black pepper (for adults)
1 heaped tbsp parsley, finely chopped
1 heaped tbsp chives, finely chopped
1 tsp olive oil
1 small knob butter

Very gently beat the eggs, adding a tiny pinch of salt (and pepper if required) and three-quarters of the chopped herbs. In an omelette pan heat the olive oil and butter until it begins to foam. Pour in the egg mixture and cook for a few seconds. Stir with a fork for a few seconds. Leave and then repeat until the eggs are cooked through. Roll the omelette and turn onto a plate. Brush with a little olive oil and sprinkle the remaining herbs on top and serve.

Quick tip:

✓ *Instead or as well as the herbs, you can sprinkle in a handful of grated cheddar cheese. Alternatively, you can add some cooked flaked salmon, a handful of cooked peas or some cooked chopped tomatoes.*

Great because:

✓ *Eggs are full of good nutrition: lots of high-quality protein, B vitamins for healthy nerves and lutein, the yellow pigment needed for helping to protect eyesight. The yolk also gives us an interesting super-nutrient called choline, which is needed for nerve and brain health.*

PUDDINGS *

My motto is, never miss an opportunity to put fruit into a pudding. It helps children to get used to the idea that what they love eating can also be good for them. Also, most fruit-based puddings look colourful so are fun to eat. The recipes here are all relatively light and much more nutritious than, for instance, cheesecake or banoffi pie!

I tend to use granulated fruit sugar in place of sugar because it has a lower GI (glycaemic index). This means that it causes less of a spike in blood sugar after eating. Also, because fruit sugar is about a third sweeter than sugar, you can use less of it. You can use ordinary sugar instead, if you prefer, but you may need to use a bit more to achieve the same sweetness.

Raspberry crush

This simple 'ice cream' could not be easier to make and is a lovely way to introduce children to new berries. As an alternative to raspberries, you can use: blackberries, when in season and picked from hedgerows; strawberries, fresh, frozen or canned in natural juice; and even apricots canned in juice. You can serve it with extra fruit on the side if you wish and with a little crisp biscuit or wafer.

> **200g raspberries (fresh, frozen and defrosted, or canned in natural juice)**
> **4 tbsp granulated fruit sugar**
> **500g Greek yoghurt or fromage frais**

Put all the ingredients into a food processor and blitz until they are combined but not completely blended. Put into freezer-proof container and freeze for about 2½ hours. At this point it should be fairly easy to scoop out and serve. Serves 12 children; 4 adults.

Great because:

✓ *Raspberries are particularly good for fibre and are packed with helpful antioxidant super-nutrients.*

Poached pears

Baked pears make a really nice light pudding. I find that half a large pear is plenty between my two little ones, but vary quantities according to your child's appetite and age. An adult can easily eat a whole pear for themselves. If you have any left over, pop it in the fridge and use it as the base of a snack for the following day.

2 firm pears, peeled, leaving stalk intact
1 small orange, grated and juiced
1 small lemon, grated and juiced
150ml red grape juice
1 tbsp runny honey

Peel the pears, leaving the stalk intact. Next, grate the zest of the orange and lemon, then juice both too. Place pears in a small saucepan with the red grape juice and the zest and juices of the lemon and orange. Bring to a brisk boil, then simmer for about an hour until the pears are tender, basting every 10 minutes. Remove the pears and leave them to cool, then turn the heat up and boil the juices until they have halved in volume. Stir in the runny honey. Cut the pears into sections appropriate in size to the age of your little ones and pour over the thickened juices. (You can serve this with a little blob of ice cream or Greek yoghurt if you prefer.) Serves 2.

Great because:

✓ *Pears have a low allergenicity, which means that most children can cope with them from an early age.*

✓ *They give us soluble fibre, which is good for our circulation.*

Apple and apricot crumble

Lots of us have our own favourite recipes for crumble, which include variations in both the topping mix and the fruits used. I like to add some small rolled porridge oats to my toppings to vary things, and when it is blackberry season, I always roll out the apple and blackberry crumble! Serve with a blob of fromage frais or plain yoghurt. Suitable once your baby is over a year of age. It can be blended if necessary.

125g plain wholemeal flour
50g polyunsaturated spread, cold from the fridge, cut into small sections
50g brown sugar
1 handful rolled porridge oats
250g cooking apples, peeled, cored and sliced
1 orange, rind grated, and juiced
250g apricots, canned in natural juice, lightly blended

Preheat your oven to 180°C/350°F/gas 4. Make the crumble topping by putting the flour in a bowl and rubbing in the spread. Once you have an even consistency of course crumbs, stir in the sugar. Peel, core and slice the apple and lay in an ovenproof dish that has a 1 litre capacity. Grate the rind of the orange and squeeze its juice. Sprinkle over the apples. Blend the apricots a little in a food blender and then lay on top of the apples. Finally, spoon the crumble mix evenly over the apricots and bake for 25 minutes or until the crumble is nicely browned. Serves 4.

Great because:

✓ *Apples give us soluble fibre, the type that helps to keep blood sugar steady, and helps to lower cholesterol.*

✓ *Apricots add some of the super-nutrient beta carotene, thought to be good for the eyes.*

Prune Pudding

* * * * * * * * * * * * *

This is a version of a recipe I found on the Californian Prunes website and which we make quite often. They use chopped prunes but for little children, I find that puréeing the prunes works really well and the children seem to enjoy it better without prune 'bits' to chew on. It will keep in the fridge for the following day when it makes a good afternoon snack as well. Serve with a plain Greek yoghurt.

800g sweet potatoes, peeled and chopped
125g soft prunes, de-stoned and chopped
3 tbsp hot water
75g polyunsaturated spread or unsalted butter
100g granulated fruit sugar (or 125g granulated sugar)
zest of 1 lemon
2 eggs

Preheat oven to 180°C/350°F/gas 4. Peel, chop and cook the sweet potatoes in a pan of briskly boiling water for about 20 minutes until cooked through. Meanwhile, chop the prunes (taking the stones out if need be) and blend with about 3 tbsp hot kettle water. Set aside. Drain and mash the sweet potatoes and mix in the butter and the granulated fruit sugar followed by the prune purée. Grate the lemon and stir in the zest. Finally, whisk the eggs and stir in to mix. Pour into a shallow baking dish and bake for 20–25 minutes. Serves 4.

Great because:

✓ *Prunes help to cut down the fat you need and give some really useful energy-boosting iron, which is also needed for normal brain development and concentration.*

✓ *Prunes are also good for natural fibre and are an age-old constipation remedy.*

Rice Pudding

· · · · · · · · · · · · ·

Like so many pudding recipes, we often have our favourite ways of making this classic, comforting one. Both of my children love it in this very simple form although you can try adding dried fruits, such as a handful of sultanas or chopped dried apricots. If you do add dried fruits, soak them first in a little water for 30 minutes; otherwise they will absorb some of the milk, which may make the final pudding a bit dry.

50g short-grain rice
1 tbsp granulated fruit sugar
1 vanilla pod or ¼ tsp vanilla essence
600ml semi-skimmed milk

Grease a 600ml ovenproof dish and preheat the oven to 180°C/350°F/gas 4. Put the rice, granulated fruit sugar and vanilla pod in the dish and then pour in the milk. You can use a drop of vanilla essence if you can't get hold of a vanilla pod. Bake in the oven for 20 minutes and then turn the heat down to 150°C/300°F/gas 2 and cook for another 1½ hours. Check to see how it is getting on. You may find that your pudding needs another 30 minutes for the rice to be nice and soft, so factor in this time just in case. Once ready it should be creamy with soft rice and a golden-coloured skin. If you have not added dried fruit to the rice pudding, you can add a blob of stewed apple and blackberry to the pudding once in a bowl. Serves 4.

Great because:

✓ *This is a filling pudding, good if your children have not eaten a large main course.*

✓ *Rice pudding is packed with bone-building calcium.*

Baked peaches

· · · · · · · · · · · · · · · ·

Peaches are a lovely soft fruit that children tend to like ripe. However, baking them gives another, deeper flavour. They go beautifully with rice pudding (page 241) or custard. If you have leftover peach, refrigerate and use the next day: try them gently puréed and stirred into Greek yoghurt at breakfast time, topped with crushed Oatibix for a bit of a crunch.

4 ripe peaches, halved and de-stoned
1 orange, squeezed (or 4 tbsp orange juice from carton)
30g granulated fruit sugar
25g unsalted butter

Preheat your oven to 190°C/370°F/gas 5. Cut the peaches in half and remove the stones. Place in a baking dish skin-side down. Choose a dish in which all 8 pieces fit snugly. Cut the orange in half and squeeze out the juice or, alternatively, use about 4 tbsp orange juice from a carton. In a small bowl, stir together the fruit sugar and orange juice and then the butter. Divide between the peaches. Bake for 15 minutes, then check how they are getting on. They will probably need 20–25 minutes in total, depending on ripeness and size. While checking, carefully scoop some of the juices from the bottom of the dish and pour back over peaches. Once soft and ready to eat, remove from the oven and put to cool. Cut into suitable-size sections for your little ones, removing the skin if necessary. Serves 4.

Great because:

✓ *Peaches give us a range of antioxidant orange and yellow pigments believed to be useful for skin and eye protection.*

Baked apples

Baked apples are a staple pudding in our house because they are simple to make and everyone enjoys them. You need to get the sweetness level right, which depends a bit on the apple itself. Adding a little granulated fruit sugar at the end can make the difference between them being enjoyed and rejected so be prepared to tinker a bit. Serve with some custard, ice cream, yoghurt or fromage frais. Older children may like some toasted chopped almonds with their dried apricots.

2 cooking apples, cored, ends sliced flat, skins pricked
1 tsp apple juice
50g dried apricots, finely chopped

Preheat your oven to 200°C/190°F/gas 6. Cut the base off each apple, slicing away just enough so that they stand up nicely and don't topple over. Remove the core and then, with a sharp knife, pierce the skin of the apple, pricking all the way round its circumference so that it won't burst when baking. Mix the apple juice and apricot pieces, dividing the mixture between the apples, and filling the centre of each. Bake for 35–45 minutes until the apples are cooked through. Remove from the oven and cool well before serving. Serves 2.

Great because:

✓ *If you can get your children to eat some of the apple skin, they will benefit from the super-nutrient quercetin, believed to help fight some virus infections. However, this may only be possible if you blend it, because they do tend to be a bit tough.*

✓ *The flesh is a good source of soluble fibre, which helps to keep blood cholesterol levels healthy.*

Healthy crème caramel

This is an easy and reasonably healthy version of a classic French pudding, which can often otherwise contain quite a lot of cream. We serve ours with chopped berries.

2 eggs
1 yolk of a small egg
60g granulated fruit sugar
250ml milk
1 drop vanilla essence
75g granulated fruit sugar
25ml water

Preheat your oven to 140°C/280°F/gas 1. Break the two whole eggs into a bowl. Next, separate the smaller-sized egg and add the yolk. (The white can be used in an omelette later in the day.) Whisk the egg, 60g granulated fruit sugar and milk together and add a tiny drop of vanilla essence. Pass through a sieve and set aside in the fridge. To make the caramel part of the pudding you need to put the 75g granulated fruit sugar and water into a saucepan and bring to the boil. Don't stir the mixture until you begin to see it thickening. When it starts to thicken and go a lovely caramel colour, pour into the bottom of 2 ovenproof ramekins and pour the egg and milk mixture on top. Place the ramekins in a roasting tray. Add boiling water to the tray until it almost reaches the top of the ramekins and then carefully place in the oven. Bake for about 40 minutes until the puddings are set. Take out of the baking tray, cover and leave to cool. Once cool, you can either serve the crème caramels in the ramekins or turn them upside down and hope that they come out in one piece with caramel dripping down the sides! Serves 4.

Great because:

✓ *It is not jam-packed with sugar yet is a sweet-tasting, protein-rich pudding.*

✓ *The milk provides plenty of bone-building calcium while the egg yolks give a little vitamin D, which helps absorption of this mineral.*

Fruit-salad jellies

· · · · · · · · · · · · · · · · · ·

I'm a big fan of canned fruit. Obviously, I don't use it all the time because I know that the taste and texture is different to fresh fruit and the vitamin levels are lower as well. But as a cupboard standby it can be really useful, especially when making jellies. Canned fruit, having been 'cooked' in the canning process, is soft and easy for children to eat.

380ml orange juice
20ml juice from the fruit salad
1 tbsp gelatine (or agar agar equivalent)
100g fruit salad, canned in natural juices

Using a small Pyrex bowl, pour in half of the fruit juice and sprinkle over the gelatine. Leave for 5 minutes and then place the bowl on top of a small saucepan containing gently simmering water. Stir the juice and gelatine until the gelatine granules begin to melt and become clear. Pour in the rest of the fruit juice. Put the fruit salad in the bottom of a 200ml jelly mould or a small flat-bottomed bowl and pour over the juice mix. Put in the fridge for about 35 minutes (leave longer if necessary) until the jelly is set. Serves 2.

Great because:

✓ *This pudding provides a lot of immune-boosting vitamin C.*

✓ *The canned fruit salad counts as a child's serving of fruit towards the 'five a day' target.*

Grape and apple jellies

You can, of course, also make jellies with fresh fruit and this recipe makes the most of black grapes, which are colourful and fun to eat.

400ml apple juice
100g black grapes, cut into quarters
1 tbsp gelatine (or agar agar equivalent)

Make as with the fruit salad jelly above. This is nice served with a blob of fromage frais.

Great because:

✓ *Black grapes are good for super-nutrient flavonoids. It is never too early to start introducing fruits, which are good for the heart and circulation.*

✓ *Apple juice provides more flavonoids. Cloudy versions contain more than the clear.*

Grilled pineapple with ice cream

This pudding is a treat for older children because it does contain a little added sugar in the recipe and, of course, in the ice cream too.

4 thick fresh pineapple rings
5g butter
10g brown sugar
4 small scoops ice cream

Put the grill on to heat and, in the meantime, melt the butter. Put the pineapple rings on some foil on a baking tray and brush with the melted butter. Sprinkle over the sugar and then grill for about 5 minutes under a medium to hot grill until the pineapple looks golden-brown. Remove from the grill tray and put each piece of pine-apple on a small plate. Let them cool down enough to be safe to eat and put a small scoop of ice cream in each of the pineapple rings to serve. Serves 4.

Great because:

✓ *Ice cream may sound naughty, but it is actually low GI, which means that it raises blood sugar relatively slowly and you don't get a huge sugar rush.*

✓ *The pineapple ring counts as one of your 'five a day' fruits.*

Berry meringue nests

This is a nice pudding for older children to help make with you because it is very, very simple. If you do not want them to have a whole small meringue nest each, just break one in half and crumble it over the berry mix to serve.

> **100g mixed berries (fresh, frozen and defrosted, or canned in natural juice)**
> **50g plain fromage frais**
> **4 small meringue nests**

All you have to do is to mix the fromage frais with the berries (the larger berries chopped into small pieces), then divide into 4 and spoon into the meringue nests and serve. It is that simple. Serves 4.

Great because:

✓ *This is another way of presenting children with vitamin C-rich fruit, which is good for their immune system.*

✓ *Berries are packed with antioxidant super-nutrients, including the 'anti-pollution' ellagic acid in strawberries.*

Banana custard with chocolate

A real comfort pudding, I remember making this with my grandma and it still makes me think of her when we eat it at home.

1 tbsp custard powder
½ pint of milk (semi-skimmed if children are over 2)
25g granulated fruit sugar
1 banana, peeled, sliced (with each slice quartered)
10g milk chocolate (optional)

Blend the custard powder with 2 tbsp of the milk and set aside. Put the remaining milk in a small pan and heat until almost boiling. Add this milk to the custard powder mix and stir well. Quickly rinse out the saucepan, then return the milk and custard mixture to it, bringing to the boil and stirring constantly. Allow to boil for 1 minute, still stirring. Add the sugar. Peel and slice the banana and chop each slice into quarters to make the right size for little mouths. Divide this banana between 4 ramekin dishes, then cover with the custard. Allow to cool down until the right temperature to serve and then, just before serving, grate a little of the chocolate over each custard pot. Serves 2 adults; 4 children.

Great because:

✓ *Custard is a good way of boosting bone-building calcium.*

✓ *You can add more banana if you wish. Half a banana will count as a portion of most children's 'five a day'.*

Plum fruit fool

* * * * * * * * * * * * *

Another easy pudding that can be made straight from the store cupboard if you usually have yoghurt on standby in the fridge. You can keep the fool in the fridge for a few days.

250g plums, canned in fruit juice and drained
1 tsp granulated fruit sugar
150g Greek yoghurt

Blend the plums until smooth and put into a bowl. Stir the fruit sugar into the Greek yoghurt and add the plum purée. Stir gently, then divide between 4 small bowls and serve. Serves 4 adults; 8 children.

Great because:

✓ *Plums are full of blue and purple antioxidant pigments, which are believed to help keep your blood vessels healthy.*

✓ *They also provide fibre, while yoghurt adds a little extra calcium for bones.*

Apricot bread and butter pudding

Another comforting and slightly more substantial pudding, this is a good way to introduce dried fruits. The fruit sugar helps to keep sweetness up but overall sugar content down. Serve with a blob of fromage frais.

2 slices wholemeal bread, lightly spread with butter
1 tbsp dried apricots, cut into small pieces
1 egg
15g granulated fruit sugar
250ml milk

Preheat the oven to 180°C/350°F/gas 4 and grease a 425ml ovenproof dish. Butter the bread and cut into triangles, arranging half of them on the bottom of the dish. Sprinkle the apricot pieces on top and then add another layer of bread and butter triangles. Beat the egg with the fruit sugar and 2 tbsp of the milk and set aside. Heat the remaining milk until it is steaming and stir in the egg mix and continue stirring for 2–3 minutes. Pass through a sieve, pouring on top of the bread and butter layers and leave to soak, covered, for 20 minutes in the fridge. Bake for 40 minutes, then check if set. You may need to leave for another 5 minutes. Once ready, you will be able to press the top of the pudding to assess if the custard is liquid or set. Remove, cool down and serve. Serves 2.

Great because:

✓ *Wholemeal bread adds fibre and some useful energy-boosting iron as well as immune-boosting zinc.*

✓ *Apricots add to these nutritional benefits giving us fibre and iron.*

CONVENIENCE FOODS *

I am not a fan of serving up fast food on a regular basis but I do think that some types can have a place in a healthy kitchen. If they make the difference between you being able to rustle up a meal or having to call for a take-out, then there is no question that they are worth having in your freezer or store cupboard.

Here I have given my top 10 list of fast foods with some ideas of how to serve them. I'm sure that you will have lots of other ideas for their uses, but it's a start at least.

1.   Frozen peas

Without doubt, one of my most important freezer standbys. The big companies genuinely freeze their peas within a couple of hours of harvesting, which means that, if you store them correctly and cook them quickly, they almost certainly have more nutrients (such as vitamin C) than fresh peas sold in supermarkets. Obviously, if you grow your own and cook them within minutes of harvesting, then fresh will be 'best', but let's be honest, most of us aren't that lucky.

At home I add frozen peas to lots of dishes: from hot pasta meals and risottos to omelettes and pasta salads. You need to be sure that your little one is old enough not to choke on them, but once they are past this stage, they are massively versatile.

I also use them to blend with avocado to make a version of guacamole (see below). It is tasty and adds some useful amounts of vitamin C as well.

Guacamole with peas

400g frozen peas
1 avocado (about 400g), flesh chopped
4 tomatoes, diced
4 small onions, peeled and chopped
4 tsp lemon juice
few drops Worcestershire sauce (optional)

Cook and cool the peas. Peel, remove stone and cut up flesh of the avocado and then dice the tomatoes and peel and chop the onions. Put the peas into a blender and blitz. Add the avocado and blitz again for a short time just so that it is broken up but not smooth. Put into a bowl and stir in the tomatoes, onion and lemon juice. If your children like it, add a few drops of Worcestershire sauce for extra flavour. Serves 4.

2.   Pizza bases

You can buy these in most supermarkets. I find them really useful when we are running late and have arrived home with little time to make dinner. You can just spread them with some homemade tomato sauce (page 183), tomato purée or passata and then top with your favourite healthy pizza toppings like slices of tomato and mushrooms with some ricotta cheese. Then into the oven to cook.

3.   Frozen white fish

Whether you opt for cod, pollock or haddock, they can be cooked from frozen in a pan with milk, adding fresh herbs to give flavour. They are ready within 15 minutes.

You can serve the fish with frozen peas and some chunks of soft bread or with some quick-cook noodles or colourful pasta shapes to make a fast and nutritious dinner.

4. Quorn sausages

These have 0.4g of salt per sausage. If you grill them and serve with some mashed potato (taken from the inside of a microwaved baking potato), along with some frozen peas, this is not a bad dinner to serve up when in a rush. You can also try them in the Sausage pasta salad below, for older children.

Sausage pasta salad

300g pasta shells (wholemeal, if your children will eat them)
120g frozen peas
100g frozen sweetcorn
100g frozen French beans
4 Quorn sausages grilled, cooled and sliced into small pieces
2 tbsp low-fat French dressing (optional)
chopped herbs (optional)

Cook pasta as directed, then drain and cool under running cold water in a colander. Cook peas, sweetcorn and beans, cool, then chop beans into 1cm pieces. Grill the Quorn sausages and chop when cool. Mix all cooked ingredients together. Add French dressing and chopped herbs if required. Serves 4.

Great because:

✓ *This colourful salad gives you a serving of vegetables for the day from the peas, sweetcorn and beans, which, along with the pasta and Quorn sausages, provides a filling and slow release of energy in the afternoon ahead.*

5.   Baked beans

If you go for the reduced sugar and salt versions, baked beans are not a bad food for children over a year old. A 100g portion has just 3g of sugar and 0.5g of salt. If you serve them on toast you need to be aware that you are adding around another 0.8g of salt so I prefer to have them on a microwaved baked potato, which is naturally salt-free. I take the potato out of its skin and serve it mashed with a little milk. Alternatively, you can mash the baked beans with the inside of the potato with a little olive oil.

6.   Fish fingers

I think it is well worth going for a well-known brand that uses a better-quality fish fillet and has breadcrumbs coloured with turmeric and paprika rather than anything artificial. I particularly like Birds Eye's 'omega 3' fish fingers because they also have some added fish oil to help boost intakes of these essential fats. A couple of good ways of serving them are below:

Fish finger wraps

2 fish fingers
2 tsp natural yoghurt
1 tsp tomato salsa
1 tortilla wrap
lettuce, very finely shredded

Grill the fish fingers and set them briefly to one side once cooked. Spoon some plain yoghurt and a blob of tomato salsa on to the middle of a tortilla wrap. Lay on top 1 or 2 fish fingers, depending on the age of your child, and a little lettuce if they can manage it. Roll up and serve. Serves 1.

Rice salad with fish

4 Birds Eye steam bags of rice, broccoli, sweetcorn and peas
12 Omega 3 Birds Eye fish fingers
2 tbsp chopped dill or parsley (optional)
1 tbsp French dressing (optional)

Cook steam bags and fish fingers as directed, then cool. Chop fish fingers into small chunks, mix together and add herbs if required. Just before serving add French dressing (optional). Serves 4.

7.   Uncle Ben's Express Long Grain Rice

This rice takes just two minutes to cook in the microwave and while it is a huge cheat and more expensive than boiling your own rice from a normal packet, it can be a great store cupboard standby. When we use it, we tend to throw in bits and pieces that need using up like some roast lamb, broccoli and carrots that failed to get eaten from the last meal. Pulses, such as canned chickpeas (which I crush down for Freddie), are good too. If I have some tomato sauce (page 183) in the fridge I also add a tablespoon of this to the rice. It gives the rice lots of flavour and colour. Other times we just add chopped avocado, cooked chicken pieces and sweetcorn, which makes a surprisingly filling and nutritious meal as well.

Although the rice has been seasoned, it contains no artificial colours, preservatives or flavours and has 0.3g of salt per 125g serving, which isn't too bad given that most young children will eat less than a full portion.

8.   Ambrosia Rice Pudding

These come in cans or individual 'yoghurt' pot-style containers; both can be stored in your kitchen cupboard. These rice puddings are great if you haven't had time to whip up a pudding and there is a feeling of 'oh no, not another fromage frais' in the air. Yes, they do have a bit of added sugar, but it is about two teaspoons per 100g. My children would share a 150g pot between them and I used it as a base to which I'd add fruit like stewed apples, canned plums or peaches. It may not be quite as tasty as the real thing, but it still gives your children a fair bit of bone-building calcium and isn't so sweet that it will distort their tastebuds forever.

9.   Canned Fruit

We always have canned fruit (in natural juices) in our cupboard at home, not least because if you happen to have run out of fresh fruit, a serving still counts towards your little one's 'five a day'. Of course, the vitamin C content in canned fruit is lower than in their fresh versions, but not all of it is destroyed in the canning process so you do still get some benefits from this immune-boosting nutrient. Canned fruit also retains its fibre (for example, in the skins of canned plums) although most canned fruit, like peaches and pears, are peeled. It does taste different too so I don't recommend it all the time. As a cupboard standby, however, it is great to have a few cans always in stock.

10. Soups

You need to be very careful with the ones you opt for because the salt levels of canned and ready-to-serve soups can be high. One I do like is the Sainsbury's Vegetable and Barley Soup because it can be frozen. It makes a really good base for quick suppers for older children if you add some extra protein like pieces of cooked chicken or some canned chickpeas. It has 0.5g of salt per 100g, but if you dilute it with the same quantity of some of your own homemade stock (page 181) or milk, this can be halved. If you are going to use canned soups, be really careful to check the salt levels and don't go for anything above 0.5g per 100g and always dilute it (with homemade stock or milk, for example) in order to reduce salt intake.

PARTY FOOD *

You may not know what your offspring are going to tuck into when going to other people's parties, but you can certainly lay on a healthy but tasty spread when it's in your home, be it a birthday party or friends coming round to play. Here are some simple offerings, which sit nicely alongside hummus (page 224) and carrot sticks and mini sandwiches.

In addition to these recipes, you can use some of the jelly recipes (pages 245 and 246) in the Puddings section as well as the carrot cake recipe (page 158) in the Breakfasts section.

If you do make sandwiches, remember that bread has around 0.4g of salt per slice so try to use fillings that do not notch this up much further. Ricotta cheese has a mild taste and spreads well; it is really nice in sandwiches with freshly sliced pieces of cucumber.

Avocado mashed to make a 'butter' that spreads easily is also a lovely, nutritious filling for sandwiches and goes well with some very finely chopped pieces of tomato. When using tomatoes for sandwich fillings it is best to slice them open, remove the seeds and watery bits, before finely chopping; that way the sandwich does not get soggy.

DIPS

Bright green dip

. . . .

Coco named this pea and mint dip 'the bright green dip' (and it sort of stuck). Given that children love colour, this green dip should get them interested and, once they've tried it, they should be coming back for more! This purée is delicious served cold as a dip but can also be heated gently in a small saucepan with a small knob of butter, plus a little milk. It can then be used as a base on which to serve fish.

> 450g good-quality frozen peas
> 20 mint leaves, finely chopped
> 2 tbsp semi-skimmed milk
> 1 tbsp plain fromage frais
> 1 tiny pinch salt
> 1 pinch black pepper

Lay the peas on a tray to defrost by 30%. Whilst peas are defrosting, blanch the mint in boiling water for 20 seconds, remove and set a side. When the peas are still very cold, place along with the mint and fromage frais in a blender and blitz until very smooth (if needed you can add just a splash of water to help). Once blitzed, push the purée though a fine sieve. Return purée to blender for a final blitz then remove and season. Serves about 10, 45g portions.

Great because:

✓ *This vibrantly colourful green dip gives your children iron, which is vital for growth, development and energy, as well as lots of vitamin C for strong immunity to help fight other children's germs!*

Chickpea and aubergine dip

A little variation on standard hummus, this dip is great for parties and children's snack times and is especially tasty with oatcake and vegetable sticks.

2 medium aubergines, rubbed with oil
1 largish shallot, finely chopped
2 garlic cloves, peeled and crushed
2 tbsp extra-virgin olive oil
80g cooked (or canned) chickpeas
½ medium lemon, juiced
75g reduced-fat crème fraiche
1 tiny pinch salt
1 pinch black pepper

Preheat your oven to 180°C/350°F/gas 4, then put the aubergines in and roast. After 1 hour remove, cut in half and scoop out the insides, which should be almost like a purée. Set aside in a dish. In a frying pan, sauté the shallot and garlic in half the oil on a medium to low heat until they start to turn golden-brown. At this point add the chickpeas and sauté for 5 minutes. Then add the aubergine mixture and continue to sauté for a further 5 minutes, stirring almost continuously. Remove from heat and set aside to cool. Put the aubergine mixture with all of the remaining ingredients in a blender and blitz until you have a purée of a good consistency for dipping. Serves about 10 children.

Great because:

✓ *This will not load your children's arteries with saturated fats and salt like many shop-bought dips.*

Tomato guacamole

This is lovely served with slices of warm, grilled pitta bread for a more substantial party food rather than just having with vegetable sticks.

1 large avocado (or 2 small), flesh diced
10g lemon juice
Tiny squeeze fresh lime juice
1 medium-sized tomato, peeled, deseeded and diced
1 large pinch fresh coriander leaves, finely chopped
25g half-fat crème fraiche

Chop the soft ripe avocado into small pieces. Add lemon and lime juice, mix well and cover with an airtight lid to avoid discoloration. Leave to stand for 30 minutes. Finely dice the tomato and add to the avocado along with the coriander and crème fraiche. Serves 4.

CHEESE AND FRUIT NIBBLES

Cheese and pineapple

Obviously you cannot give cocktail sticks to young children but, instead of impaling the cheese and pineapple pieces, serve them together on the same plate This way they make an excellent finger food where children can still enjoy the combination of creamy cheddar and zingy pineapple.

100g medium-mature cheddar, cut into small 10g cubes
75g pineapple, cut into small cubes (if using canned, opt for those in natural juices)

Simply put the small pieces of cheese and pineapple on a plate, well mixed to encourage children to try them together. Serves about 2–3 children depending on age and appetite.

Ciabatta pizzas

See page 198. Make up and serve some lovely ciabatta pizzas with your children's favourite toppings.

Jewelled couscous

You can make this more filling (and use as an ordinary hot or cold main course for children) by adding: pieces of cooked roast chicken, beef or pork; flakes of cooked salmon, which is good for younger children who still need softer food (all bones carefully removed); or some crumbly cheese such as goats' cheese (only use a little of the latter, however, because it is rather salty. A little goes a long way in terms of flavour).

250ml homemade stock (page 181) or water
1 tbsp olive oil
200g couscous
1 small knob butter
1 handful black grapes, cut into quarters and deseeded
1 medium-sized tomato, deseeded and finely chopped
1 tbsp sweetcorn (canned or frozen, cooked and cooled)

Pour the stock (or water) into a pan. Add the oil and heat gently. Once hot, add the couscous and stir with a wooden spoon. Cover with a lid, remove from the hob and leave for about 3 minutes until all the liquid has been absorbed. Add a small knob of butter and return to the heat with the lid on and simmer gently for a further 3 minutes. Remove, put into a bowl and separate grains by passing a fork through the couscous. Cover and allow to cool, then put in the fridge. When ready to serve, add the grapes, tomato pieces and sweetcorn. Stir and serve. Serves 4.

SWEET TREATS

Pear and pecorino cheese

· ·

This is Franco's Italian take on cheese and pineapple, which is totally delicious!

100g pecorino cheese, crumbled on a plate
1 hardish pear, cut into easy-to-hold pieces (peel for younger children)

Let them pick at the pieces as with the pineapple and cheddar. This Italian version makes a lovely change and is very tasty.

Apple crumble cake

· ·

This is lovely cake, which uses fresh fruit and is best eaten within two days of making. With any remaining dough, roll out with a rolling pin and use to make biscuits.

For the base:

140g plain flour
140g self-raising flour
75g granulated fruit sugar
2 small eggs, lightly beaten
90g unsalted butter, melted
3 apples (preferably Pink Ladies), peeled, cored and cut into eighths
180g blueberries (you can use other berries or chopped dried fruits)

For the crumble:

> **80g unrefined sugar**
> **10g melted, unsalted butter**
> **10g plain flour**
> **2 tsp cinnamon powder**
> **icing sugar to dust**

Sift flours and fruit sugar into a mixing bowl and whisk together for a minute or so, then stir in the beaten eggs and melted butter. Slowly mix ingredients until you have a smooth dough. Remove dough from bowl. Take two-thirds of the dough and press into a 26cm spring-form cake tin, greased and lined with baking paper, then arrange your apples close together on top of the mixture. Sprinkle over blueberries. Set aside whilst you make the crumble.

For the crumble:
Preheat your oven to 190°C/370°F/gas 5. Put all your crumble ingredients into a food processor and and pulse thoroughly until well combined. Scatter the mixture evenly over the apples and blueberries. Next, take 25g of the remaining dough and roll marble-sized pieces into small balls. Use to cover the crumble. Finally, bake for 70 minutes, depending on your oven. You are looking for a golden-brown finish. If the crumble begins to brown too quickly, loosely cover with some greaseproof paper. Sprinkle lightly with icing sugar to serve. Serves 10.

Great because:

✓ *Most cakes contain very little fruit, but this one has a good serving of apples and blueberries, which are rich in antioxidant super-nutrients, which are not destroyed on baking, to help boost your children's all-round health and immunity.*

Raspberry Granita

This is nice served in a small bowl garnished with a blob of ice cream and a raspberry.

750ml red grape juice
130g granulated fruit sugar
1 sprig fresh mint
400g fresh raspberries
12 extra-fresh raspberries

Empty grape juice into a medium-sized saucepan and add the granulated fruit sugar and mint. Bring to the boil. Make sure the fruit sugar has completely dissolved. Add the raspberries and turn off the heat. Leave for 1 hour in the saucepan. Then, remove the mint leaves and pour raspberry mixture into a blender. Blitz until raspberries have completely broken down and the mix is consistent in texture. If you want a finer texture, you can, at this point, sieve the mixture. Empty into a shallow freezer-proof container. Place in freezer. Remove and stir the granita thoroughly every 30 minutes to stop too many ice crystals forming. Continue to do so for 3 hours. Serves 12 children.

Great because:

✓ *This is a low GI pudding, which means that it keeps blood-sugar levels steady so that you won't have children bouncing off the walls.*

✓ *Raspberries are packed with ellagic acid, a super-nutrient that is believed to fight pollution. They also give us some vitamin C, which boosts immunity.*

Berry skyscraper

. . . .

Once your pudding is in the fridge, the sugar soaks into the yoghurt top layer, making it delicious to eat, while the other layers all develop their own flavour.

80g granulated fruit sugar
350g Greek yoghurt
110g of your favourite berries (strawberries, raspberries or blueberries)
4 tsp unrefined brown sugar (or more, to taste)
4 tsp grated lemon rind

Stir half the fruit sugar into the Greek yoghurt and the other half into the berries. Put layers of berries and Greek yoghurt into plastic see-through cups. Make the final layer a yoghurt one and sprinkle over a little brown sugar on each. Allow to sit in the fridge for a few hours. Serves 12 children.

Great because:

✓ *Berries are great for immune-boosting vitamin C.*

✓ *This pudding is also bursting with purple antioxidant pigments in the blueberries, which are thought to be good for circulation.*

Mini apricot scones

· · · · · · · · · · · · · · · · · · ·

The heart and diamond shapes you can create make this an ideal party food.

200g self-raising flour
25g sugar
½ level tsp salt
30g butter
2 tbsp ready-to-eat apricots, chopped
50g dried apricots, chopped
125ml milk

Preheat your oven to 230°C/450°F/gas 8. Sift the flour into a mixing bowl and stir in the sugar and salt. Add the butter and cut into small cubes. Lightly rub the fat into the flour mixture. Once a light mixture has formed, stir in the apricots. Make a well and pour in the milk. Fold flour crumble and once roughly mixed, with clean hands, finish forming a dough ball. On a floured surface gently roll dough until 2cm thick and use shaped cutters to make mini scones. Bake 8–10 minutes. Cool and serve. Serves 12.

Great because:

✓ *These are lower in sugar and fat than many traditional party cakes but are fun to eat and naturally sweet-tasting because of the apricots.*

Banana bread

A wonderfully sustaining snack when you have children round to play. You can butter it or simply cut it into bite-sized squares.

75g butter
100g granulated fruit sugar
2 eggs
450g bananas (peeled weight), mashed
200g self-raising flour
¼ tsp bicarbonate of soda
½ tsp salt

Preheat oven to 180°C/350°F/gas 4. Grease and line an oblong loaf tin (about 8 inches by 4 inches). Cream the butter and sugar. Add the eggs and beat well. Add the bananas and beat again. Add flour, soda and salt. Pour into cake tin. Bake for 75 minutes. Turn onto wire rack and let cool before cutting.

INDEX

Recipes are in **bold.** Brand names are in *italics.*

baked apples 243
baked beans 254
baked potatoes 173
bananas
    mashed banana 121
    apple, pear and banana purée 141
    avocado and banana purée 141
    banana bread 268
    banana custard with chocolate 248
    blueberry and banana purée 142
    grilled bananas with fromage frais
        152–153
batch cooking 6
beef
    basic mince 210
    Bolognese sauce 206–207
    cottage pie with carrots and peas 209
    meatloaf 206
    perfect steaks 210–211
beetroot and potato purée 133
berries (*see also* blackberries; blueberries;
    raspberries; strawberries)
    berry meringue nests 247
    berry skyscraper 266
    fromage frais and berry layers 171–172
    frozen berry yoghurt 170
beta carotene
    improved availability through cooking 72
    in organic produce 58–59
    as 'super-nutrient' 16
    and vitamin A 15
bitter tastes
    generally 3, 34–35
    broccoli 35, 118
blackberries
    apple and blackberry lollies 171
blueberries
    apple crumble cake 263–264
    blueberry and apple purée 137
    blueberry and banana purée 142
BMI (body mass index) and conception 95–96

Bolognese sauce 206–207
bottle feeding 13
bread (*see also* ciabatta; pitta bread; rye
    bread)
    fillings (for potatoes, wraps, bread) 173
    not before 6 months of age 109
    not overloading on wheat 19, 20
    salt in 18
    wholegrain cereals 20
breakfasts
    importance of 148–149
    low salt breakfast cereals 18, 26
    for mums 81–83
    recipes for 150–159
    salty cereals 18
    weaning breakfasts 111
breastfeeding
    between 6–12 months 13, 147
    exclusive for 6 months 13
    and food allergies 46
    nutrients in breastmilk 14–17
broccoli
    broccoli purée 118
    broccoli and pea purée 130
    broccoli and chicken quick risotto 223
    sautéed broccoli with garlic 234–235
    sweet potato and broccoli purée 135
    too bitter for some tastes 35, 118
bruschetta 231–232
BSE (mad cow disease) 59
bulgur wheat
    bulgur wheat with apricots 228
    Moroccan chickpea casserole with
        bulgur wheat 226
Bush, G. and the broccoli ban 35
butternut squash purée 116

caffeine 76–78, 89
cakes
    apple crumble cake 263–264
    apricot and chocolate muffins 150–151

Notes

· · · · · · ·

Notes

Notes

Notes

Notes

Notes

Notes

Notes

Notes
· · · · · · ·

HAY HOUSE TITLES OF RELATED INTEREST

Baby to Toddler Month by Month,
by Simone Cave and Caroline Fertleman

The Bloke's Guide to Babies,
by Jon Smith

How to Stop Your Kids Watching Too Much TV,
by Teresa Orange & Louise O'Flynn

L Is for Labels,
by Amanda Ursell

Time Management for Manic Mums,
by Allison Mitchell

What Are You Really Eating?,
by Amanda Ursell

JOIN THE HAY HOUSE FAMILY

As the leading self-help, mind, body and spirit publisher in the UK, we'd like to welcome you to our family so that you can enjoy all the benefits our website has to offer.

 **EXTRACTS** from a selection of your favourite authors' titles

 **COMPETITIONS, PRIZES & SPECIAL OFFERS** Win extracts, money off, downloads and so much more

 **LISTEN** to a range of radio interviews and our latest audio publications

 **CELEBRATE YOUR BIRTHDAY** An inspiring gift will be sent your way

 **LATEST NEWS** Keep up with the latest news from and about our authors

 **ATTEND OUR AUTHOR EVENTS** Be the first to hear about our author events

 **iPHONE APPS** Download your favourite app for your iPhone

 **HAY HOUSE INFORMATION** Ask us anything, all enquiries answered

join us online at **www.hayhouse.co.uk**

 292B Kensal Road, London W10 5BE
T: 020 8962 1230 E: info@hayhouse.co.uk

ABOUT THE AUTHOR

© Gerald Rambert

Amanda Ursell is a qualified nutritionist and has a diploma in dietetics. She is also an award–winning journalist, television presenter and author.

Born and brought up in West Sussex, England, Amanda studied at King's College London where she gained a 2:1 BSc degree in Nutrition and the Associateship of King's College (AKC). She was President of the Student Nutrition Society, and on completion of her degree course spent a further year at King's to be awarded a postgraduate diploma in Dietetics.

With weekly columns in *The Times* and *The Sun* newspapers, and monthly articles in *Healthy magazine*, *Healthy Food Guide* and *Spirit & Destiny magazine*, she is the most widely read nutritionist in the UK.

As well as regularly presenting on the *Tonight* programme, she was also GMTV's nutritionist for 13 years and has presented various television series including *Food File* and *Eat Up*, both for Channel 4.

She is a member of the British Dietetic Association, the Nutrition Society and the Guild of Food Writers, and has been made a Visiting Fellow of Oxford Brookes University.

In 2003 Amanda was awarded the HFMA Health Writer of the Year award, and in 1999 and 2000 was voted the most influential health professional in the UK.

www.amandaursell.com